Riverfront
PROPERTY:

Connecting at the River of Life

Steven C. Johnson

BurkhartBooks
www.burkhartbooks.com
Bedford, Texas

DEDICATION

Treasured Lamb of God,
You are the dearest One,
our good Shepherd,
so worthy of glory, honor and power!
May You somehow receive this imperfect manuscript
as a fragrant offering.
May it be Your pleasure to reveal Yourself
through it so many will connect with You
at the riverfront!

Contents

PRIMER

This book is motivated by the conviction that history is about to be hijacked by Heaven. For the past two thousand years followers of Yeshua (Jesus) have been praying, "May Your kingdom come on our planet just as it prevails in the highest Heaven." A colossal answer is bulging above us and about to splash forth with the Return of the King!

Anticipation stimulates preparation. What grander project can there be than preparing a landing strip for our Monarch? I pray Riverfront Property will stimulate those longing for His coming – those preparing the way.

It's heartening to see little signs and wonders demonstrating this venture is birthed from His heart. Our daughter Claire had a dream where I was working in a huge library. I was studying about water and was preparing to make a presentation. I told Claire in the dream she too should study about water. On another occasion a young prophetic friend told me, "God has given you 'a roar' like rushing water." One woman said Pam and I are like deep wells with fresh, clean water. No one knew I had been working on this project.

You are about to discover two distinct "rivers of life". One refers to a future, tangible watercourse flowing out of a city you find on a map, Jerusalem. You will be able to travel to this river, dangle your feet in it and swim there. Fruit trees will drink from the river. You may walk the shore munching their delectable produce!

"The river of life" is used in another sense, as an inner spiritual river—the Holy Spirit given to those embracing Yeshua. This spiritual river transports us into joy and purpose and glory! You will realize dynamic transformation and empowerment through its gentle stillness, and mighty surging!

It is not enough to enjoy this river alone. Many live in Death Valley, shriveled by dehydration. Our lives cannot be complete until we learn how to be conduits and imparters of the river's dynamism. There is satisfaction for ourselves, and blessing for others, as we communicate this river.

Wherever this river flows things will live! Its resurrection life is welcome news to millions! We are everlastingly grateful to The River Master. This book is ultimately about knowing and walking with Him by the riverfront. He is the guide for both the outer, tangible river and the inner, spiritual river. As you read on and comprehend this river you may find it a complement when someone says, "You're all wet!"

The one thing this book lacks is the dynamic interaction possible in the Riverfront Property Seminar. Learning about the two rivers of life and how to navigate those streams comes much easier when in good company. If you can't make a conference I suggest you read Riverfront Property with a group of friends who know, or long to know, the liquid realities of, "Christ in you."

For those who must read the last chapter first to find the conclusion let's save some page flipping. When they ask, "What was the book about? What did you learn?" you may answer,

**"Follow the Lamb
and He will lead you to the Waters of Life."**

For the Lamb at the center of the throne will be their shepherd; He will lead them to springs of living water. And God will wipe away every tear from their eyes.

- Revelation 7:17

Episode 1:

WATER REFLECTIONS

JESUS AT THE WATERSIDE

Would it surprise you to discover Yeshua loved living at Peter's home on the north shore of Galilee?

Did He relish the sunrise glinting on the water and the thunderstorms pelting and dotting the lake? Did Jesus love to see the wind ruffle Peter's sail? Was he entranced as he looked back at the wake following the boat? Perhaps He was too spiritual....

Not at all! Remember Jesus is the one who told Nicodemus to be aware of the wind and who told the crowds to notice the lilies and the birds, and the disciples to treasure the children!

Like us, He was mesmerized by the water lapping at the hull and rocking the boat. Do you suppose Jesus was a swimmer? He couldn't have been afraid of the water! Can you imagine our Lord stripping down with the guys and taking the challenge of racing out to Andrew's boat?

There were plenty of trials in Messiah's life and ministry but still, Jesus is the expert at wringing pleasure out of simple things. He loves to be around the water. Of course he does unusual things with it. He turns it to wine! He walks on it! Picture His tongue-in-cheek smile.

After a day of scrambling over the stony shore following and listening to their astonishing Rabbi what did they do for dinner? Perhaps they barbequed fish with Peter's patented seasoning mix. There was joy on the lake!

JUST ADD WATER

Want to see kids have fun? Just add water! Do you want to cultivate romance? Add a walk by a wooded stream or sandy beach. There are those who love the wilds of the desert but most prefer a vacation or picnic outlined by water.

I shiver with longing when I drive by an ocean, lake or river. I desire water like a fish! Water soothes and invigorates, calms and activates! How refreshing to splash, dive and swim in the wet! Let me paddle, sail or ski over it. Let me simply dangle my feet in it!

Have you taken a boat cruise, gone white water rafting or tubed behind a speed boat? What fun! Have you gone deep sea fishing? Don't you love it! We can tell God loves H2O. He made so much of it! He gave birth to water.

> *Does the rain have a father? Who fathers the drops of dew? From whose womb comes the ice? Who gives birth to the frost from the heavens when the waters become hard as stone, when the surface of the deep is frozen?*
>
> *- Job 38:28-30*

One of the first things you see in Scripture is God's Spirit reverberating and resonating over the waters. There was a miraculous induction of purpose into the deep. As the Spirit hummed, and strummed, and reverberated things came alive!

So please, add the water so the fun and romance may begin!

GETTING SOAKED

Were you born land-locked and never learned to swim? Are you afraid of the deep end, never venturing out over your head? I had a fear of water as a child. As I learned to swim fear diminished. I still have a respect for the deep.

The summer after third grade my parents did a cruel thing. They forced me to join swim team. Why would parents subject their children to miles of exhaustion? I literally tried to hide when swim practice came because it was so doggone hard. I resented the water like a wet house cat. Funny, some things parents force us to do end up becoming loves.

On one childhood vacation our parents rented a little houseboat and we spent a handful of days on a lake in Wisconsin. I was magnetized by living right on top of the water! In my growing-up days enjoyment increased as we lived beside a lovely lake and near splendid rivers. There is no better way to get your eyes open in the morning than by looking out over a body of water!

My ambition in high school was to be a professional water skier. I say in good humor, "The older I get the better I was!" It was exciting to ski jump, spin on trick skis and even fly in a kite behind a boat. I was able to barefoot ski and do tricks with the driver's help, like skiing around the boat. The most invigorating thing was to cross the wake doing sixty and make deep strong turns.

Long hours of canoeing made me comfortable with a paddle. When our son was ten we were in a family camp canoe race. Parents were blindfolded in the back seat of the canoes. Children gave directions from the front seats. Because I know how to keep a canoe going pretty straight without looking Brian just had to do a little touch up in the front and tell me how we needed to turn.

I play memories of sitting pleasantly becalmed in our

homebuilt sailboat, the Sea Hag. I also remember three friends hiking out on the catamaran as we cut through chop doing 22 knots. The hull was humming and the stays were singing with vibration. Thrilling! Sailboat races are in my memory treasure chest.

Over time my relationship with the deep moved from fear of drowning, to wet-cat resentment, and on to comfort, adventure, exhilaration and delight.

Do you keep distant from what you cannot fathom, apprehensive of the denizens of the deep? Is it fear of floundering or getting your hair wet? I suggest a good squirt-gun fight to break the surface tension. There is still time to make memories - by going out over your head. Let's get soaked and venture into the deep end!

FOR SALE: RIVERFRONT PROPERTY

Living by the water in my early years had a "magical" quality. I have had too little contact with open water in recent decades, and get home sick. One of my therapies is to swim three days a week. It helps stave off the longing for the deep.

From time to time I find myself flipping through the ads, scanning for riverfront property, a place on a river to call home. It's beyond my financial reach and unrealistic, but the magnetism keeps pulling. What if …how wonderful it would be… to dwell by the water again!

Birds sense an intuitive urge to find their way home. My instinctual ache, my intuitive pining, is to return home and find my place by the river! Do you feel it; the impulse, the longing, to return to Eden and the river which sprang up there?

Search the web for "River of Life" and you will find millions of references. "River of Life" has been published on the billboards of thousands of congregations. It is the theme of songs and sermons. Followers of Jesus refer to it, but it seems the truths of this river are only vaguely known.

"What can you tell me about the river of life?" I've spent a couple decades pondering this river yet every time I ask the question I learn something new.

There is One who holds the answer to all mysteries. Let's inquire of Him for revelation.

Dear Heavenly Father,

You are the Spring of Life!

You are the Revealer of mysteries.

We humbly ask You to uncover the secrets of Your river.

Lamb of God, lead us to streams both outward and tangible, and inward and transformational.

Romance us, captivate us, by the river.

We long to learn more, to experience more of Your power, love, wisdom and purpose.

Make us conduits of Your liquid life for those who may not even realize they thirst.

For the splashingly wonderful things You disclose, we give thanks!

Rivers are made of vast congregations of water molecules. What is in a droplet?

ENGINEERING THE WATER MOLECULE

Water is the most amazing chemical! We should tremble every time we hold a cup of it. It's used for leveling and lubricating, tempering and dissolving, cooling and heating. Some even bathe in it! It comes in three manifestations. We harness its power to mill our flour and brew our coffee.

Water has other important functions. It is for stomping on in puddles. It's for splashing and for squirting. God our Father, the great, creative, chemical Engineer, did a walloping job in designing water. There are more complex chemical compounds but none so plentiful and intriguing as dihydrogen monoxide, that is, water.

You can hardly call the water molecule boring. The Oxygen and Hydrogen atoms do a wildly exotic dance. Their do-si-dos are much faster than you can blink. Every millisecond, every one thousandth of a second, they swing atoms to trade partners. Water is not a static element but lightning quick!

This magnificent molecule is smaller than a light wave so we can't see its inner machinery. We can deduce some of its qualities, such as its triangular shape. Do you ever have that "clumpy" feeling as you drink down those three-cornered molecules? Where does water's slippery texture come from? Rather mysterious.

Water, unlike most molecules, expands when frozen. What would we do if ice sank to the bottom of lakes and oceans? The molecule can act like an acid or a base. We can separate water electro-chemically into hydrogen and oxygen. When we burn the elements the product of combustion becomes water again!

Two thirds of our planet is covered with it. There are gazillions of these molecules. If the earth was perfectly round and smooth the depth of the water would be 9,000 feet. No wonder Noah's boat cleared the underwater mountains in the day of earth's calamity.

Here is yet another reason to worship our Creator. See how He designed the perfect surface tension for H2O. If it were lighter it would not bead and fall as rain. If it were stronger we could be clobbered by one gallon rain drops!

Like the earth's surface most of our physical composition, about 65%, is water. If you were a jellyfish it would be 95%. Lord forbid we be dry personalities!

THE PROBLEM OF THIRST

You wake in the night with cotton mouth and a tongue like leather. You are thirsty! A tall glass of water and you feel human again. We all have a little experience with thirst.

What would you do if you turned on the faucet but there was no water? Do you have a few gallons stored for an emergency? Do you have a lake, stream or well nearby? Could you purify water by filtering, boiling, or with chlorine? You may have a stocked pantry but if you don't have the ability to access clean water you are in trouble! Thirst is not a philosophical or theoretical problem.

Water is sorely missed when absent or polluted. We are in a world of hurt without $H2O$! Dehydration shuts down our digestion. The blood thickens. The heart labors. Our urine darkens. We become feverish. Unless we get rehydrated we are facing a parched death.

The ancients probably valued water more than we do. Even today some trudge miles to find it.

There is a story of primitive people who visited our nation and after seeing our technological wonders where asked what most impressed them. They said water coming out of a pipe amazed them most!

Water makes it to market with a price. Some have predicted it will become more valuable than oil. In some places it already is. When we were in Kenya water was delivered by truck or donkey cart. I choked tears at the airport in America where we got fresh, clean water, with ice, for free!

Hell's fire is pictured as a place devoid of moisture, with a miserable longing for just a drop of water. Millions today have more than an idle interest in water. They long for it with a parched, withering desperation. Who will satisfy their need? Perhaps you are part of the answer.

Our Lord Jesus, the One who said "I thirst", is also the One who leads us to living waters! We don't think of water as having taste but when we are parched it tastes delicious! Consider the kindness of God. He sends rain on the righteous and the unrighteous.

GOD'S HEART TO SATISFY

Our Creator generously satisfies our thirst!

Psalms 107:9 tells the lost desert wanderers,

> *Let them give thanks to the LORD for his unfailing love and His wonderful deeds for men, for he satisfies the thirsty and fills the hungry with good things.*

Psalms 104:10-11 tells us God gives

> *...water to all the beasts of the field; the wild donkeys quench their thirst.*

Our gracious God never intended for people to be oppressed by drought. His heart is to satisfy the thirsty. He even has a bucket blessing!

> *Water will flow from their buckets; their seed will have abundant water.*
> - Numbers 24:7

HUNGER AND THIRST ARE ANSWERED IN JESUS!

The thirsty get a dose of prophetic assurance in Revelation 7:16-17.

> *Never again will they hunger; never again will they thirst. The sun will not beat upon them, nor any scorching heat. For the Lamb at the center of the throne will be their shepherd; He will lead them to springs of living water. And God will wipe away every tear from their eyes.*

Never hungry! Never thirsty! Living water is the refreshment given those who follow the Lamb.

> *He leads me beside quiet waters.*   - Psalm 23:2

The Lamb, who is also our Shepherd, will lead us to comforting, refreshing waters!

God tosses in another blessing—a tear-free eternity! (Isaiah 25:8; Revelation 21:4) Pain, regret and death are wiped away along with our tears!

I suggest you let Revelation 7:17 make a big impression. Engrave it or whittle it into your imagination. You might take a card and write it out to post on your bathroom mirror or fridge. Absorb its reality. This is good news! Our thirst finds its quenching because of the Lamb!

> *For the Lamb at the center of the throne will be their shepherd;He will lead them to springs of living water. And God will wipe away every tear from their eyes.*

The Jewish prophets tell us about the river of life which

will spring from Jerusalem. Our Jewish Messiah Yeshua will lead us by that riverside. To provide context we look now to Israel and their waterworks both ancient and modern.

ISRAEL'S WATER SYSTEMS ANCIENT AND MODERN

It would be fascinating to climb into a time machine and observe life in ancient Israel. But to study archaeology and dig through ruins is plenty exciting! I had the privilege of studying in Jerusalem back in 1974. Our group uncovered antiquities from the time of Christ at the south end of Herod's Temple mount. We discovered large baths called mikvahs used for ceremonial purification. Before entering the temple area the religious would bathe in the mikvahs. The Christian practice of baptism finds its roots there.

In those pools we discovered artifacts, lamps and pottery. What an eerie, thrilling thing to uncover mysteries which have been buried in darkness for generations! Those lamps once glowed in the hands of their owners. One can't help wonder about their names and faces, their joys and troubles.

Jerusalem averages 26 inches of rain yearly. There are six months without rain so when it returns there is celebration! Some places in the south, like the desert of Zin get only a couple inches yearly. In the far north, Mount Hermon fares better, getting 45 inches. Water systems have been integral to sustain the population of ancient Jerusalem which was often in the hundreds of thousands, swelling to the millions during holy festivals. Where was water found for bathing, drinking, washing and cultivating?

I'd love to take you on a tour of Israel and show you ancient water systems. How tremendous to stroll through places where biblical characters walked thousands of years ago! We would visit Warren's shaft, a water tunnel which David's men may have used three thousand years ago to capture the Jebusite city, and make it his capital. (1 Samuel 5:8)

Old and young are fascinated as they wade through the waters of Hezekiah's tunnel. It was carved to protect the water supply from the siege of Assyrians seven hundred years before Messiah. (2 Kings 20:20)

We would look at the water conduits to the Temple and the ceremonial baths. You'd be awed with the aqueducts of Herod! They ran from miles away in the hills of Hebron and Bethlehem to Jerusalem. They also ran to the Dead Sea providing for palaces and gardens in the desert.

In Herod's day "PVC pipes" were carved from stone. These were coupled together to channel water down and then back up hills. Those ancients were clever! Can you imagine how labor intensive, to carve pipes and keep them sealed for pushing water up hills!

You should see the pool of Bethesda on Jerusalem's north where Jesus healed the lame man. On the south you would be impressed with recent excavations at the Pool of Siloam. Jesus sent the blind man there to gain his sight.

Yes, I do think you would enjoy a tour of Israel, where people, with names and faces, long ago cut channels through stone, and dug ponds and cisterns. When would you like to visit?

WATERWORKS IN ISRAEL TODAY

Israel is like children arguing over a toy which was ignored, until one child picked it up and started playing with it. No one wanted Israel. Since it has been made beautiful and prosperous everyone wants a piece.

In 1800 only a couple hundred thousand lived in Israel. Now the young, reborn nation is going on eight million! The land was stark and deserted. Today Israel has been cultivated and beautified! The barren land of a hundred years ago is now sought after.

Prophecy is being fulfilled; the desert has been turned to garden!

> *The desert and the parched land will be glad; the wilderness will rejoice and blossom. Like the crocus, it will burst into bloom; it will rejoice greatly and shout for joy. The glory of Lebanon will be given to it, the splendor of Carmel and Sharon; they will see the glory of the LORD, the splendor of our God.*
>
> *- Isaiah 35:1-2*

Today the Israelis are experts in conserving, transporting and metering out water. Much of the land is still waste but so much has been reclaimed! There are striking "before and after" pictures where the wilderness has turned to savannahs of grass, and to forests. You may drive by miles of farms, fruit groves and greenhouses that just a few decades ago were uncultivated desolation.

Modern Israel has battled water shortages since its rebirth in 1948. Out of necessity amazing technologies have been created. They don't squander water for frivolous things like washing cars. In the dry season most cars are covered with dust. We used a bucket to sponge bath ours!

Most of Israel's water supply comes from Mount Hermon and the rainy north. Those waters infiltrate the soil creating the headwaters of the Jordan River. The beautiful Sea of Galilee is the nation's chief water reservoir. Waters exiting Galilee continue south down the Jordan. Most of it is captured for good purpose before reaching the Dead Sea.

The nation capitalizes on their limited resource stretching their potential with drip irrigation and water reclamation. They aid developing nations through the export of water technologies.

Rain and snow are not sufficient to meet the nation's demands. Israel is the leader in water desalination. The world's largest reverse osmosis desalination plant is in Ashkelon providing 165, 000 cubic meters of water per day. This plant filters drinking water from the Mediterranean providing thirteen percent of Israel's domestic needs.

A land that was ignored for centuries is again blooming like a rose through the care of her modern residents!

All this is background. Now let's turn to a puzzling verse of Scripture.

Episode 2 :

THE TANGIBLE RIVER

THE MYSTERY OF PSALM 46:4

"There is a river whose streams make glad the city of God, the holy place where the Most High dwells."

Psalm 46 beautifully reminds us,

God is our refuge and strength, an ever-present help in trouble.

Because He is we can be fearless in the face of earthquakes and tsunamis. We can be still and know, "He is God." In contrast to the earthquake the Psalm tells us

His holy place is unshakable, because He is there. We are also told a river with streams is there. This is puzzling!

If you travel to Jerusalem you may look high and low but there is no river to be seen! Yet King David says, "There is a river whose streams make glad the city of God, the holy place where the Most High dwells?" In rainy moments there are little rivulets in Jerusalem but nothing to label a river.

Where is this river which makes the city glad? The closest thing to a river is an occasional creek which trickles down the Kidron Valley between the Temple mount and The Mount of Olives. But if it is not raining don't strain yourself to find it.

At the southern, lower end of David's original city there is the artesian Gihon spring. It flows at perhaps four gallons a second. It is hardly what we would call a river with streams. Gihon spring provided water for the Pool of Siloam. Israel's kings were dedicated at the pool. The spill-off watered orchards and gardens.

Back to the mystery, how David said,

> *There is a river whose streams make glad the city of God.*

Was there a river flowing when David wrote Psalm 46? The closest thing to a river would have been the tiny seasonal Kidron brook or the little Gihon spring. 2 Samuel 15:23 mentions David crossing over the Kidron brook as he fled from Absalom. Perhaps it was raining.

Years later in 70 AD the Roman Army may have gathered water for themselves at the Kidron as they besieged the city. But on a hot August day everything is dry.

What did David mean when he said,

> *There is a river whose streams make glad the city of God, the holy place where the Most High dwells?"*

I am convinced David was speaking prophetically of a river we will yet see spring from the rocky ground of the old city. David wrote of a river with streams, plural. We know of streams which flow into rivers to enlarge them. The only time I am aware of a river producing streams is in the first garden. Remember?

> *"A river watering the garden flowed from Eden; from there it was separated into four headwaters. The name of the first is the Pishon; it winds through the entire land of Havilah, where there is gold. (The gold of that land is good; aromatic resin and onyx are also there.) The name of the secondriver is the Gihon; it winds through the entire land of Cush. The name of the third river is the Tigris; it runs along the east side of Asshur. And the fourth river is the Euphrates."*
>
> - Genesis 2:10-14

My Friend, David was speaking prophetically of a future river that would produce multiple streams and make the city of Jerusalem glad! The Hebrew prophets will demonstrate this, but for a few moments let us take our camera lens and go panoramic.

THE ULTIMATE NEW WORLD ORDER

Momma Cass sang, "There's a new world coming." How right she was! Our glorious anticipation is the return of the King. Jesus promised if He went away He would also return. He will return to Jerusalem and be King of Kings and Lord of all earthly Lords. He will not return in a vague mystical sense but in His concrete, palpable, resurrected body! What a day!

It is important to see the kingdom as a tangible, physical reality. Many have conceived the kingdom as a vaporous, fanciful dreamland where we strum harps on clouds. The fact is Heaven is breaking forth on earth in tangibility!

A day is coming when our Lord Jesus Christ will return to our planet and answer our 2000 year old prayer, "Thy kingdom come on earth." Attended by multitudes of angels His feet will come down and touch the Mount of Olives east of Jerusalem. Valleys will rise up. Mountains will get humble and melt like hot wax. There will be great geological changes.

He will shape Jerusalem as the capital of the whole earth. He will rule the earth with an iron scepter. Talk about authority! Many watch the news from Israel today. Then, the entire planet will focus on Jerusalem, the city of the Great King.

The days of waiting will be behind us. To finally see Him face to face will be inexpressible joy! Resurrection! Restoration! The Renewal of all things! Those will be the Bride Groom days of Consummation, the perfect happily-ever-aftering! Jesus our Anointed One will be with us! Emmanuel! This reality is the most wonderful of rapturous thoughts for those who love the One called, The Desire of All Nations!

Revelation 21:3-4 says,

Now the dwelling of God is with men, and he will live with them. They will be his people, and God himself will be with them and be their God. He will wipe every tear from their eyes. There will be no more death or mourning or crying or pain, for the old order of things has passed away.

What an amazingly dreadful and wonderful day it will be when Jesus takes his throne to judge! We certainly want to be ready! We could spend years probing the mysteries of the new world – the glory of God, streets of gold, gates of pearl, the 24 elders and the cherubim. Our focus is a river.

A QUARTET OF PROPHETIC INSTRUMENTS

The Scriptures are peppered with references to streams and fountains which reflect the river of life. As you read your Bible you will find dozens of passages which allude to what Psalm 36:8 calls, "the river of delights."

For our purposes we highlight a special quartet of Scriptures which frame this great river. Let us introduce you to Joel, Zechariah, Ezekiel and John in Revelation. Listen to a sound bite from each of them.

A fountain will flow out of the LORD's house.
- Joel 3:18

On that day living water will flow out from Jerusalem, half to the eastern sea and half to the western sea.
- Zechariah 14:8

I saw water coming out from under the threshold of the temple.
- Ezekiel 47:1

Then the angel showed me the river of the water of life, as clear as crystal, flowing from the throne of God and of the Lamb.
- Revelation 22:1

We will expand our reading of these four passages but as we begin consider geographically where this river originates.

Out of the LORD's house...   - Joel 3:18

Out from Jerusalem...   - Zechariah 14:8

From under the threshold of the temple...
- Ezekiel 47:1

From the throne of God and of the Lamb...
- Revelation 22:1

Let's pull with our ears to comprehend the harmonies of these four prophets'.

JOEL SOUND HIS NOTES

"In that day the mountains will drip new wine, and the hills will flow with milk; all the ravines of Judah will run with water. A fountain will flow out of the LORD's house and will water the valley of acacias.

- Joel 3:18

"That day" in the Bible is also called "the day of the Lord." If you wish to get a tremble and sense of exhilaration study those expressions! That day, when God has His way, things will be changed! Joel forecasts a fountain originating in the Lord's house and proclaims water will go down into the valley of acacias. Acacia trees grow in the arid places east of Jerusalem. They are very durable. Joel says the dry valley will become a watered valley! The ravines will run with water, all because water will come out of the Lord's house!

ZECHARIAH STRUMS HIS STRINGS

Zechariah's strings will rock your boat! First he talks about warfare and devastation coming to Israel. Then the Lord comes to the rescue! His feet stand again on the Mount of Olives and the world is changed!

[1]A day of the LORD is coming when your plunder will be divided among you. [2]I will gather all the nations to Jerusalem to fight against it; the city will be captured, the houses ransacked, and the women raped. Half of the city will go into exile, but the rest of the people will not be taken from the city.

- Zechariah 14:1-2

This scenario has tragically happened under Babylonian and Roman rule. Will it happen again? What has never happened is revealed in the following verses.

> *³Then the LORD will go out and fight against those nations, as he fights in the day of battle. ⁴On that day his feet will stand on the Mount of Olives, east of Jerusalem, and the Mount of Olives will be split in two from east to west, forming a great valley, with half of the mountain moving north and half moving south. ⁵You will flee by my mountain valley, for it will extend to Azel. You will flee as you fled from the earthquake in the days of Uzziah king of Judah. Then the LORD my God will come, and all the holy ones with him. ⁶On that day there will be no light no cold or frost. ⁷It will be a unique day, without daytime or nighttime—a day known to the LORD. When evening comes, there will be light. ⁸On that day living water will flow out from Jerusalem, half to the eastern sea and half to the western sea, in summer and in winter. ⁹The LORD will be king over the whole earth. On that day there will be one LORD, and his name the only name.*
> *- Zechariah 14:3-9*

WHERE DOES ZECHARIAH'S RIVER GO?

According to Zechariah the river flows west through gullies and channels and eventually enters the Mediterranean Sea. Likewise it flows east through wadis and fissures until it comes to the Dead Sea.

Wadis are dry creek beds which occasionally flood

from rain. Far down the slopes in the desert wilderness wadis suddenly fill with accumulated rain which has fallen miles up the hills. These wadis become raging rivers and deadly traps for unsuspecting hikers. People are drowned on sunny clear days as water rushes down these dry, narrow gullies catching them by surprise.

If you look at a satellite image of Israel you see Jerusalem as a highpoint between the seas. Water from Jerusalem has the opportunity to flow either east or west just as a rain drop at the top of our American Rocky Mountains can divide and flow east or west.

Now we could track the water flowing to the west, for those waters will be welcomed, but I am far more interested in tracing the water to the east. The west typically gets moisture from the Mediterranean rains and is fruitful. The Jerusalem ridge route is a barrier preventing rain from getting to the east side. Consequently you can stand on a high point in Jerusalem and looking to the west you will see green, but when you turn to the East you see desolation.

As you move east there is something unique. The barren slope goes lower and lower.

You descend from Jerusalem 2500 feet to reach what would be sea level on the Mediterranean. You pass sea level signs but you go down another 1385 feet before you reach the Dead Sea. You have descended nearly 4000 feet! The Dead Sea is a geographic wonder, the lowest spot on earth. You are now in the Jordan valley, part of the Great Rift Valley which runs deep into Africa.

What do you know about the Dead Sea? The Dead Sea gets its name for a reason. Nothing lives there! The water has a 32% salt saturation. You can't sink in the Dead Sea. People love to float high in the brine getting their pictures taken reading newspapers. Just don't get any water in your eye. It burns like crazy! Nothing can live in the Salt Sea.

The Kidron brook back in Jerusalem runs south and then east through miles of twisty fissures to the Dead Sea. This passage is called in Arabic Wadi-en-Nar, the Fire Wadi. It reminds me of Daniel 7:10 where it says,

> *A river of fire was flowing, coming out from before Him.*

As we pick up Zechariah again we see the passage is not talking about a mystical, imaginary river. These places are on the map.

> *The whole land, from Geba to Rimmon, south of Jerusalem, will become like the Arabah. But Jerusalem will be raised up and remain in its place, from the Benjamin Gate to the site of the First Gate, to the Corner Gate, and from the Tower of Hananel to the royal winepresses. It will be inhabited; never again will it be destroyed. Jerusalem will be secure.*
>
> — Zechariah 14:10

EZEKIEL ADDS HIS HARMONY

The Scriptures teach the resurrection of the dead. How

far can God's resurrection power reach? According to Ezekiel even the Dead Sea will be raised to life! Wherever this river flows things will live!

¹The man brought me back to the entrance of the temple, and I saw water coming out from under the threshold of the temple toward the east (for the temple faced east). The water was coming down from under the south side of the temple, south of the altar. ²He then brought me out through the north gate and led me around the outside to the outer gate facing east, and the water was flowing from the south side. ³As the man went eastward with a measuring line in his hand, he measured off a thousand cubits [1500 feet] and then led me through water that was ankle-deep. ⁴He measured off another thousand cubits and led me through water that was knee-deep. He measured off another thousand and led me through water that was up to the waist. ⁵He measured off another thousand, but now it was a river that I could not cross, because the water had risen and was deep enough to swim in—a river that no one could cross. ⁶He asked me, "Son of man, do you see this?" Then he led me back to the bank of the river. ⁷When I arrived there, I saw a great number of trees on each side of the river. ⁸He said to me, "This water flows toward the eastern region and goes down into the Arabah, where it enters the Sea. When it empties into the [Dead] Sea, the water there becomes fresh. ⁹Swarms of living creatures will live wherever the river flows. There will be large numbers of fish, because this water flows there and makes the salt water fresh; so where the river flows everything will live. [10]Fishermen will stand along the shore; from En Gedi to En Eglaim there will be places for spreading nets. The fish will be of many kinds-- like the fish of the Great Sea. [11]But the swamps and marshes will not become fresh; they will be left for salt. [12]Fruit trees of all kinds will grow on both banks of the river. Their leaves will not wither, nor will their fruit fail. Every month they will bear, because the water from the sanctuary flows to them. Their fruit will serve for food and their leaves for healing.

- Ezekiel 47:1-12

This river enlivens the region into a lush, fruitful, prosperous habitat.

JOHN, THE LAST MEMBER OF OUR QUARTET, SOUNDS OUT

[1]Then the angel showed me the river of the water of life, as clear as crystal, flowing from the throne of God and of the Lamb [2]down the middle of the great street of the city. On each side of the river stood the tree of life, bearing twelve crops of fruit, yielding its fruit every month. And the leaves of the tree are for the healing of the nations. [3]No longer will there be any curse. The throne of God and of the Lamb will be in the city, and his servants will serve him. [4]They will see his face, and his name will be on their foreheads.

- Revelation 22:1-4

All four members of the quartet have sung to us of a remarkable river which springs from the Lord's house, from Jerusalem, His temple, His throne. David also told us of this river with streams that comes from the city of our God. Five prophets tell of this river's genesis. Other prophets like Isaiah describe the river in action.

ISAIAH'S ENRICHING HARMONY

¹The desert and the parched land will be glad; the wilderness will rejoice and blossom. Like the crocus, ²it will burst into bloom; it will rejoice greatly and shout for joy. The glory of Lebanon will be given to it, the splendor of Carmel and Sharon; they will see the glory of the LORD, the splendor of our God. ³Strengthen the feeble hands, steady the knees that give way; ⁴say to those with fearful hearts, "Be strong, do not fear; your God will come, he will come with vengeance; with divine retribution he will come to save you." ⁵Then will the eyes of the blind be opened and the ears of the deaf unstopped. ⁶Then will the lame leap like a deer, and the mute tongue shout for joy. Water will gush forth in the wilderness and streams in the desert. ⁷The burning sand will become a pool, the thirsty ground bubbling springs. In the haunts where jackals once lay, grass and reeds and papyrus will grow. ⁸And a highway will be there; it will be called the Way of Holiness.

- Isaiah 35:1-8

When was the last time you saw rivers flow on barren

heights? Listen to a few more measures from Isaiah.

¹⁷The poor and needy search for water, but there is none; their tongues are parched with thirst. But I the LORD will answer them; I, the God of Is-rael, will not forsake them. ¹⁸I will make rivers flow on barren heights, and springs within the valleys. I will turn the desert into pools of water, and the parched ground into springs. ¹⁹I will put in the desert the cedar and the acacia, the myrtle and the olive. I will set pines in the wasteland, the fir and the cypress together, ²⁰so that people may see and know, may consider and understand, that the hand of the LORD has done this, that the Holy One of Israel has created it.
— Isaiah 41:17-20

HOW BIG IS THIS RIVER?

How large is the river that will flow from Jerusalem? Do you imagine something a few dozen feet wide? This river which starts ankle deep expands! The prophetic orchestra sings out a substantial river!

We know it is a river of length because it has at least two tributaries running from Jerusalem to both the eastern and the western Seas. But does it have width and depth of volume?

Ezekiel waded well over a mile down the watercourse before getting over his head. At that point he no longer advances forward but does make a mention of its width. "Now it was a river that I could not cross, because the water had risen and was deep enough to swim in-a river that no one could cross." (Ezekiel 47:5)

Interestingly Isaiah 33:21 says,

> *There the LORD will be our Mighty One. It will be like a place of broad rivers and streams.*

Just watch what happens when Jesus steps on Olivet! The city will be split both north to south and east to west. New canyons are formed. It might interest you to know Jerusalem has geologic fault lines running both north and south, and east and west.

Zechariah indicates that Jerusalem is raised up! It seems a plain flattens out along with a valley through the rocky hills. It starts in Geba 1.5 miles north of the city to Rimmon 10 miles south. Plenty of space for a river to flow!

Revelation 16:19 says the city is split into three parts. Imagine a huge cross-shaped division. We can assume the river will fill the fissures created by earthquakes then break off into other streams. Remember David said this is a river which has or produces streams! The river expands with new tributaries. This sounds more dynamic, larger than your backyard creek.

This River with Streams is not petite. John said the river flowed down a "great street." Perhaps it is a really great street with a truly great river! Maybe we need to think of this river as Amazon big!

With the Israelis' penchant for water systems we can imagine the great advantage they will take of the waters. Irrigation systems will run north and south as well as east and west to make the nation into a great garden!

THE TREE OF LIFE

The expression "tree of life" occurs eleven times in scripture starting in Genesis 2. According to Ezekiel and Revelation this tree makes a huge comeback!

> *I saw a great number of trees on each side of the river.*
> - Ezekiel 47:7

> *On each side of the river stood the tree of life.*
> - Revelation 22:2

What we were forbidden to eat in Eden because of sin we are welcome to in the fullness of the Kingdom! How lovely to walk among orchards of trees by the river! Consider yourself a happy tree if you are planted by the stream of life! Remember Psalms 1:3:

> *He is like a tree planted by streams of water, which yields its fruit in season.*

This tree is unique. Each month it produces different fruit! Are you under the weather? Chew on a leaf, apply one to a sore or make them into a tea. The leaves heal whole nations! What we witness is the restoration of the Garden of Eden. We are back to mankind's first mission, expanding Eden's borders. And there is plenty of water to irrigate with!

INSTANT RIVERS

Have you ever seen an instant river? All of a sudden

out of the ground comes a river! At Black Butte, Oregon you find the Metolius River pop out of the ground. It suddenly bursts from a hillside, and presto, we have a river! Several streams begin this way in Israel. The Harod Stream, which Gideon and his three hundred drank from spouts out of the earth. From the rocky slopes at Tel Dan there percolates waters which fuel the Jordan River. There is a gorgeous instant river at Caesarea Philippi which suddenly pours out of a hillside.

WHERE DOES THE WATER COME FROM?

Where does Jerusalem's river get its water? In many places on earth you may put down an auger and discover water. There are waters below the city of Jerusalem, in fact recently a large aquifer was found as excavators were digging to build a new high speed train.

We can speculate about how the river may spring from underground sources but remember God is the miraculous Creator and Provider of water. He may use underground sources but He can create water from nothing just as he created the earth from the invisible. He can even make water pour from a rock!

Our Father can get water from a spoken word! He can distill it from the atmosphere or even bring it from another dimension, from heaven itself! Astronomers recently discovered the largest reservoir of water ever, roughly 140 trillion times the volume of Earth's oceans. It is out of town, roughly 12 billion light years from Earth. There is no shortage of water in the universe.

How exciting to think of Israel's future abundance

where the deserts are cultivated and bloom like a rose! Nations will finally acknowledge God's sovereignty over the city, eat of the fruit and drink deeply.

But here is the most exciting thing…

THE RIVER MASTER WILL BE THERE!!!

> *For the Lamb at the center of the throne will be their shepherd; He will lead them to springs of living water. And God will wipe away every tear from their eyes.*
> - Revelation 7:17

No longer through a mirror dimly, but face to face! Imaging walking by this river, munching on delicious fruit, and doing it with The Lord of Life! Isn't that the best! How thrilling to be with him!

John the Baptist proclaimed,

> *Look, the Lamb of God that takes away the sins of the world!*
> - John 1:29

Jesus played the sacrificial Lamb for us at His engagement at the cross. We revel in His victory! Jesus' resurrection is our promise of life. Romans 4:25 says,

> *He was delivered over to death for our sins and was raised to life for our justification.*

Latch onto that!

We His sheep will be led by the Lord Jesus, the Lamb! Shepherd and Lamb rolled into One! Quiet waters, restored souls! To have the physical companionship of Jesus in a parched desert is greater than any majestic river without Him! But how grand to have Jesus and His river besides! To have Jesus as your eternal companion is everything. He is the ultimate Friend, great Counselor and Bridegroom. To know Him is life eternal! Do I have room for more exclamation marks?

WHEN WILL THIS RIVER FLOW?

No one can say definitively when the river will start flowing. Timing seems to be connected to geological turmoil, war in the land and the Lord Jesus again standing on the Mount of Olives. One thing we see is a whole lot of shaking! We have prophecies telling us the Lord will shake heaven and earth, prophecies of every wall falling down and of Zion becoming the highest mountain.

The prophecies of David in Psalms, of Joel, Zechariah, Ezekiel, Revelation and Isaiah all indicate earthquakes are part of the package.

Isaiah tells us water will flow as towers fall.

In the day of great slaughter, when the towers fall, streams of water will flow on every lofty hill. The moon will shine like the sun, and the sunlight will be seven times brighter, like the light of seven full days, when the Lord binds up the bruises of his people and heals the wounds he inflicted.
                                          - Isaiah 30:25-26

Joel tells us there will be trembling.

> *The LORD will roar from Zion and thunder from Jerusalem; the earth and the sky will tremble.*
>
> — Joel 3:16

Our planet's twenty five mile thin egg shell is going to crack and move about. I wonder if you will be one of the mountain movers.

Perhaps rather than being afraid of earthquakes you will hear God's intentions, and know His timing for them. Perhaps you will be an earth shaker joining the voices of other saints, saying, "The time has come, let the earth shake to the glory of the Lamb!"

> *I tell you the truth, if you have faith as small as a mustard seed, you can say to this mountain, 'Move from here to there' and it will move. Nothing will be impossible for you.*
>
> — Matthew 17:20

A FANCY TICKLED

I have a thought that tickles my fancy. Perhaps I'm all wet but I wonder if this river from Jerusalem will begin to spring forth preceding the coming of Yeshua.

Will Jerusalem's river suddenly burst forth at the return of Messiah, or might it start slowly and progressively increase as the people of God pray it into fullness, in preparation for the King's return? Wouldn't that be a fine sign and wonder to impress the Jewish nation and witness to the world?

In the summer of 1999 there was a surprising flow of water under the temple mount in Jerusalem beneath the foundation. Reports said it was impossible to locate the source or to stop the flow. Jewish Rabbis were intrigued. The Muslims who have possession of the temple area felt it was a bad omen.

What is stopping God from opening a spring of water anywhere in the earth for those who cry out for it? He's done it before!

Remember God told Moses,

> *I will stand there before you by the rock at Horeb. Strike the rock, and water will come out of it for the people to drink.*
>
> - Exodus 17:6

Moses struck the rock and water flowed to quench a nation's thirst.

Samson was dying with thirst after a battle with the Philistines. God heard his cry and opened up a life-saving spring of water.

> *Then God opened up the hollow place in Lehi, and water came out of it. When Samson drank, his strength returned and he revived.*
>
> - Judges 15:19

Elisha had the minstrel play and the thirsty army dug trenches. Water filled them, their lives were saved and they overcame their enemies! (2 Kings 3:4-24) In each case God sent water in unexpected ways, bringing salvation.

We know at some juncture in history Christ's new world order will come where there is no sickness or death and all tears are wiped away. But isn't the kingdom making advancements every day when people repent toward Yeshua, when the sick are healed and when demons are cast out? The last sickness and demon may not have been dealt with by the time our Lord comes, but what if we can have ten thousand times more progress, accelerating as the time draws draws near?

The job given our progenitor Adam still needs to be pursued. The nations may not be thoroughly filled and cultivated for the purposes of the Redeemer, but we can have much more of the glory of God on this half of eternity than we presuppose.

David's prophecy of a river with streams will be realized either progressively before Messiah's return or slam-bang at his coming. Either way it will be a great sign and wonder.

> *I will show wonders in the heaven above and signs on the earth below.*
>
> - Acts 2:19

OUT OF THE NAVEL

Why does Jerusalem get such center stage international news coverage?

If you had a business which required you to fly to all the cities of the earth Jerusalem would be a great place to live. It is near the geographic center of the earth - on the surface. According to Jewish tradition, the temple foundation stone is the holiest spot on earth. It is the site of the binding of Isaac, and the site of the Holy of Holies. It is the connection point between heaven and earth and referred to as the "umbilical cord." Rabbinic tradition teaches Jerusalem is the center or navel of the earth.

As the navel is set in the centre of the human body, so the land of Israel is the navel of the world... situated in the centre of the world, and Jerusalem in the centre of the land of Israel, and the sanctuary in the centre of Jerusalem, and the holy place in the centre of the sanctuary, and the ark in the centre of the holy place, and the foundation stone before the holy place, because from it the world was founded.
- Midrash Tanchuma, Qedoshim

Out of the center, from Jerusalem, the holy city, many things are about to materialize. One of them is a river with streams, which will make not just a city but the whole earth glad!

GOING ELASTIC

Have you had a good stretch? Reach for the skies because we are going to get still more elastic!

There is another stream called, "The River of Life." It is just as real as the future physical river. It emerges from within those who believe in the Lord Jesus Christ! In our next episode we will taste the wonders of that inner river!

**Follow the Lamb
And He will lead you to the Waters of life.**

For the Lamb at the center of the throne will be their shepherd; He will lead them to springs of living water. And God will wipe away every tear from their eyes.

\- Revelation 7:17

Episode 3 :

DISCOVERING THE RIVER WITHIN

HOLY ROLLERS

When I was a lower-classman at Center Street Elementary school a neighbor frightened me. Our walk to school took us by a little white church. He told me "holy rollers" met inside. He said they shouted and rolled on the floor, jumped on the pews and swung from chandeliers. Naturally I was horrified. In fact, when I walked past the building I walked faster. You never know what dreadful things might happen if you linger!

I attended a church that told me that Jesus was sweet and kind but I didn't get much more. I was part of a congregation that sadly had a pastor so deceived that he did not believe Jesus rose from the dead. I didn't come to know the Savior in a church.

My last year in high school a friend told me that Jesus was coming back. This was both disturbing and stimulating. I began to read the New Testament. Jesus seemed to be such an attractive and powerful person! My last month in High School a man told me, if I confessed Jesus as my Lord and believed in my heart that God raised Him from the dead I would be saved. I would have eternal life! (Roman 10:9-10) I remember no rockets in air or bombs bursting in air. I do remember a distinct peace and sense of bedrock security when I said, "Yes" to Him.

As a new believer I voraciously read the bible and began to connect with others that were riding on the Jesus movement of the early 70's. I found fellowship with other young believers at a Christian coffee house and also in a college ministry.

I told friends that I would love to go back in time and walk with the Lord Jesus. They told me, "No, it's better this way because Jesus has gone to heaven and has given us His Holy Spirit." I had no personal knowledge of the Holy Spirit. True, we did have some "warm fuzzy" experiences sharing together but I would have traded them in an instant to be face to face with Jesus. Jesus might be known. I wasn't sure about the Spirit. Then I was ambushed!

CHOIR PRACTICE

I was part of the choir and came to church, not knowing practice was canceled. I saw a light on in the fellowship area but found it vacant. I walked through the dark hall to the sanctuary's double doors and cracked one open. There was no light except for what came from the street outside. I thought, "Maybe I should go in and pray", at the same time I thought, "I have a lot of homework to do." In that moment of indecision I was gripped at my chest as if an invisible hand grabbed a fistful of my shirt. I was literally pulled into the sanctuary about a dozen feet! I stood in the dark room totally astonished. I laid my left hand on a pew and then received another surprise. How do I put it into words? I felt a power like electricity or surging water going through my body. Had I not been holding the pew I might have fallen. I felt holy awe!

My greatest "spiritual experience" up to that time was a sense of joy as I sang praise songs at the local Christian coffee house. This was off the grid, out of any paradigm or speculation about spiritual things! I stood still and silent. After a few minutes I felt drawn to one of the wooden lecterns up front. I walked to it and placed my hands on either side. Again, suddenly, unexpectedly this electric-water feeling came over me, and again if I had not been holding on I might have fallen. There were no words but I felt I was beginning to perceive His voice.

Had I become... a holy roller?

LIVING WATER FROM HUMAN TEMPLES

Ezekiel said a river will flow out of the temple. Rivers also flow from human temples. When the Hebrews referred to "living water", they were talking about water that flowed, water on the move. Living water comes from above and flows down. Living water is active, fresh and carries power.

Jesus keys us into the inner river.

> "Whoever believes in me, as the Scripture has said, streams of living water will flow from within him."
> - John 7:38

Does this river pour out of you?

SHARING TESTIMONY

I am so appreciative of the Holy Spirit's ministry! I would love to swap stories! My experience in the River has included:

- Times of deep conviction
- Uncontrolled laughter, as well as tears
- Wisdom and knowledge beyond myself
- Seeing the sick recover and demons driven out
- Exhilarating love!
- The physical sensation of the weight of God's glory

We have seen the power of God literally, not figuratively, raise the dead!

There was an unforgettable two hour encounter where I felt like a puppet on God's strings. It involved a sequence of "birthing", of stretching, wrestling and boxing. It was so embarrassing, and yet so fortifying! I had difficulty talking for about ten days afterwards. If you had witnessed this I am sure you would call me a holy roller.

Through streams of dreams and visions and prophetic words I have discovered God does not speak in monotone!

RIVERS TELL STORIES

I consider it an honor to have someone share their story with me. Have you ever listened to a river tell a story? I would like to read stories like this.

- The Deer Who Came to Drink
- The Stick that Traveled to the Sea
- The Fish who Swam Up Stream
- The Otters Take a Vacation
- The Garden at My Banks

A RIVER FROM A PAW-PRINT

CS Lewis grabs the river by the tail, or the tale, in his Narnia series.

In "The Silver Chair" Jill needs to come to a river to quench her terrible thirst but to do so she must come before the great lion, Aslan, the Christ figure.

In "The Voyage of the Dawn Treader" Lucy, Edmund and Eustace find the most delectable river at the ends of the East. A Lamb is there who serves them a breakfast of fish. He then turns into the Lion.

In "The Horse and His Boy." Aslan reveals himself to poor dejected Shasta and then vanishes. Shasta is caught in wonder and doubt:

"'Was it all a dream?' wondered Shasta. But it couldn't have been a dream for there in the grass before him he saw the deep, large print of the Lion's front right paw. It took one's breath away to think of the weight that could make a footprint like that. But there was something more remarkable than the size about it. As he looked at it, water had already filled the bottom of it. Soon it was full to the brim, and then overflowing, and a little stream was running downhill, past him, over the grass.

"Shasta stooped and drank—a very long drink—and then dipped his face in and splashed his head. It was extremely cold, and clear as glass, and refreshed him very much."

SHARING RIVER STORIES

Our story and purpose is revealed and finds context in The River. This is where it would be helpful to have a few friends to jam with. Can you find some?

If you feel you have little experience with the Spirit don't be discouraged. We all want to know him better. If all we do is share our desire to know the Spirit, we are leaning in the right direction.

Sharing heaven-born experiences with others primes our faith and gets us pumping! Have you had any of these experiences?

- Irrepressible joy
- Boldness to share Christ
- Deep groaning in prayer
- A sense of God's weighty presence
- Profound love or peace
- A feeling like electricity or rushing water
- Insight you knew wasn't from your smart little brain
- God's voice through dreams or visions
- The ability to supernaturally speak in another language or interpret languages
- Discernment of angels or demons
- The holy fear of the Lord
- Healings or miracles

I suggest you take time to journal your encounters with the Holy Spirit. Do not worry if you do not have monumental experiences like the dividing of the Red Sea. Consider "everyday" graces, things as simple as remembering to return a library book.

LIFE'S MATTERS AS LIQUIDS

Light, wisdom, the fear of the LORD, romantic love, peace and justice—Scripture uses fluid, river language to describe them all! We often talk of matters as if they were liquid.

- They immersed themselves in Civil War history
- They gush with generosity
- They overflow with creativity
- She surges with resentment
- He was streaming with tears
- Compassion welled up within her

Liquid language is used to describe the Spirit" raining" down or being "poured" out. Life is moving when it is liquified! Liquids can get though small openings. A little weather-stripping will not stop a flood from drenching your home. The grace of God will seep through even tiny cracks.

SEEING THE INVISIBLE

Have you sat with your hot cup of coffee or tea and been mesmerized by the tiny clouds of moisture evaporating into nothingness? As children we thought that the invisible meant nothing. We had not learned that air is transparent, yet made of tiny particles. Perhaps as adults we know better. We have even humbled ourselves enough to conceive of different dimensions of which we may be oblivious.

Our bodies are not equipped to perceive higher and lower light spectrums. We don't sense sounds above or below our hearing range. We are oblivious to radio and TV waves going through our bodies. Perhaps a few of us can sense changes in barometric pressure. Can you?

We don't have the natural equipment to see invisible realities, or do we? I am convinced that God is eager to disclose hidden things to those who seek Him.

REPRESENTATIONS OF THE SPIRIT

OIL – Prophets, Priests and Kings were commissioned with olive oil poured over the head - a symbol the Holy Spirit would rest on them. Honored guests were welcomed with oil on the head. In the 23rd Psalm, the Shepherd's Psalm, even the sheep had oil on their heads to trap ticks and flees and mites. Messiah is Hebrew, and Christ is Greek, but they both mean Oil Slathered One, One on whom the Holy Spirit rests.

FIRE – John the Baptist said in Luke 3:16, "He will baptize you with the Holy Spirit and with fire." You may remember on the day of Pentecost tongues of fire rested on the Saints. Have you felt this consuming, passionate fire?

WIND – We stayed in Netanya, Israel where sea breezes off the Mediterranean hit the sandy banks pushing the wind upwards. Colorful parasails move up and down the coast lifted by the winds. We have ridden those kites up, up and away, over the tall apartment buildings. It reminds me of 2 Peter 1:21; "For prophecy never had its origin in the will of man, but men spoke from God as they were carried along by the Holy Spirit." We can soar when the wind of the Spirit is under our wings!

WINE – Jesus gives us New Wine. We are told not to be drunk with natural wine but to be filled with the Holy Spirit! Many who come out of drug and alcohol abuse testify that the reality of the Spirit's love and power produced a greater "high" than any substance they tried.

WATER: THE DOMINANT EMBLEM OF THE SPIRIT

The prominent physical emblem of the Spirit is water. "Water" and "Spirit" are linked from Genesis to Revelation. Water surrounded us in our mother's womb. It is the same when we are born from above. Now, you may be born again but not be aware of the Spirit's waters. We are exploring that today!

ARE YOU THIRSTY ENOUGH TO ASK?

Let us convert our thirst into prayer as did King David.

As the deer pants for streams of water,
so my soul pants for you, O God.
My soul thirsts for God, for the living God.
When can I go and meet with God?

- Psalm 42:1-2

O God, you are my God,
earnestly I seek you;
my soul thirsts for you,
my body longs for you,
in a dry and weary land
where there is no water.

- Psalm 63:1

Father,
We lay hold of Your willingness to be found. May
we know You, as You are, and not just as we have
conceived You.

*We seek a true and authentic relationship with
Your Holy Spirit. Cause Your river of revelation
and illumination to stir us. Quench our thirst by
revealing Your glory and kind intentions in Your
Son, Jesus Christ our Lord.*

EXPERIENCE WITH GOD IS A MUST!

Just as expressions of love and devotion confirm rela-
tions between members of a family, true biblical spiri-
tuality must have expressions to prove it genuine. It is
essential that believers have heaven-born encounters
with God. Those experiences may bring correction, in-
struction and guidance, peace and comfort. All of these
are gifts from the Father of Lights.

Healthy families have communication, healthy bodies
have good circulation. Shared testimonies get the blood
moving. We become sensitive, recognizing His ways.
Swapping river stories builds us up. All to say - get a
circle of friends and swap accounts of Christ's love and
power. Share, listen and rejoice! See what happens. The
Holy Spirit likes to join conversations that honor God!

Cultures develop around rivers, lakes and water holes.
We connect with other "River People", forming river so-
cieties.

A KINDLY WARNING

Before we go much farther I want to present an important warning. Our long term destination is the bliss
of Eden but do not presume encounters with the Holy
Spirit are a Panacea for your problems. In fact, walking

in the Spirit adds a new batch!

Many think, "If only I could see a miracle, have a vision or speak in tongues—all my problems would go away. As believers in Christ we have incredible benefits, but the not-so-tiny print says we signed up for hardships and tribulations as well. Do not be fooled. You will be rich with extra blessings, but expect perplexity and persecution as part of the package.

AUDACIOUS LOVE

The Love of the Father is the most scandalous truth. To many it is only a rumor. Some hear the cold data; "God is love", but fewer have had the river wash that truth into their senses. So here is what you do. Fill up the bathtub with the following words, get in and marinate.

I have loved you with and everlasting love. With loving kindness I have drawn you.
- Jeremiah 31:3

The love of God has been poured out in our hearts by the Holy Spirit who was given to us.
- Romans 5:5

You are my loving God! - Psalm 144:2

Linger in the tub. After you have a good soaking you may find people surprisingly loveable, even those you do not typically get along with.

WHO IS THE HOLY SPIRIT?

Is it too late to ask the question, "Who is the Holy Spirit?" Like the Father and Son, the Spirit has many names. He is Helper, Comforter, Counselor, Guide, the Giver of gifts and character, the Imparter of wisdom and revelation. The Spirit of God is too Big to be defined. He defines us!

Just as God condescended to squeeze Himself into a temple of stone, He compresses himself into human temples who say "yes!" Christ is in us, the Hope of Glory!

The Holy Spirit is the invisible God moving among us and in us! He is the breath of God. He Leads us into the truth, reminds of things we must remember and empowers us to action. He emboldens us with His presence. He testifies to the glory of Jesus!

The Holy Spirit has been the martyr's security. He is the seal of our Salvation, our Engagement Ring and the Substance of the kingdom. We treasure Him and pray that we would never grieve or quench the Spirit, but rather stir up the waters.

On one of His many post-resurrection visits Jesus was sharing a meal with His disciples. He told them, "Do not leave Jerusalem, but wait for the gift my Father promised, which you have heard me speak about. For John baptized with water, but in a few days you will be baptized with the Holy Spirit." (Acts 1:4-5)

One hundred twenty of them took Yeshua at His word. They rejoiced, waited and prayed in an upper room for the promise. It came ten days later.

WHAT HAPPENED ON PENTECOST?

You may read in Acts 2 of the amazing account of Pentecost. The disciples got soaked! It seemed to be a cacophony of joy with a sound of a mighty wind, flames of fire resting on their heads, the ability to speak in other languages, and boldness to testify about Jesus. As you read Acts you find other occurrences where the Good News of Jesus was shared, people believed, and the river flowed!

Do you think Yeshua should have given a heads up to His disciples? He did not tell His disciples what to expect. He simply told them to wait.

Jesus could have said, "Guys, just to give you a heads up, when the Spirit comes you will:

   A. Hear a mighty blowing wind
   B. See tongues of fire resting on your heads
   C. Speak the praise of God in languages you have never learned. Some people will think you are goofy drunk.
   D. All kinds of people will respond to your message.

Here is what happened on Pentecost:

   A. The gift of circulation between heaven and earth
   B. The gift of illumination to reveal the greatness of God
   C. The gift of communication so others would comprehend

D. The gift of inspiration to captivate others for the Savior

Circulation, Illumination, Communication and Inspiration are Heaven's Objectives.

JESUS INVITES THE THIRSTY

Jesus told the woman at Jacob's well, "If you knew the gift of God and who it is that asks you for a drink, you would have asked him and he would have given you living water. Everyone who drinks this water will be thirsty again, but whoever drinks the water I give him will never thirst. Indeed, the water I give him will become in him a spring of water welling up to eternal life.
- John 4:10, 13-14

Isaiah echoes Jesus' invitation and promise to satisfy our thirst!

Come, all you who are thirsty, come to the waters; and you who have no money, come, buy and eat!
- Isaiah 55:1

They will neither hunger nor thirst, nor will the desert heat or the sun beat upon them. He who has compassion on them will guide them and lead them beside springs of water.
- Isaiah 49:10

The LORD will guide you always; he will satisfy your needs in a sun-scorched land and will strengthen your frame. You will be like a well-watered garden,

like a spring whose waters never fail.
- Isaiah 58:11

In the opening lines of Revelation John has an experience of hearing a voice behind him like a trumpet. He describes it like the voice of rushing waters! The voice is that of the exalted, radiant Jesus! The intensity of the moment makes John fall at the feet of Jesus like a dead man.

There are times where we see Jesus raise His voice. He does so at the Feast of Tabernacles where he shouts to the crowds, "If anyone is thirsty, let him come to me and drink. Whoever believes in me, as the Scripture has said, streams of living water will flow from within him."

The words are simple. Jesus must have raised His voice to drive the point home and to reach the edges of the crowd. He wanted them to know that literally all of us may come, all who are thirsty.

John explains:

> *By this he meant the Spirit, whom those who believed in him were later to receive. Up to that time the Spirit had not been given, since Jesus had not yet been glorified.*
> - John 7:37 & 39

Jesus broadcasted a thirst-quenching opportunity, an exceptional drink! He gave this invitation in different words both macro to the crowds and micro to individuals.

We were all given the one Spirit to drink!
- 1 Corinthians 12:13b

Want to be drinking buddies?

Whoever believes in me, as the Scripture has said, streams of living water will flow from within him.
- John 7:38

The phrase "within him" comes from the Greek word koilia. It means cavity and is particularly used of the abdominal cavity. Sometimes it is figuratively spoke of as the heart or belly or womb. Jesus proclaims with a shout, if we believe in Him we can expect streams of living water to flow out of our inmost beings, out of our bellies!

THE SOURCE OF THE INNER RIVER

Do you remember this song?

"What can wash away my sins?
Nothing but the blood of Jesus.
What can make me whole within?
Nothing but the blood of Jesus.
O precious is the flow that makes me white as snow.
No other fount I know,
Nothing but the blood of Jesus."

A Roman soldier stood at the foot of the cross. Jesus' phenomenal death had just taken place. The words, "Into Your hands I commit my spirit!" were the last echo. "Are you sure he's dead?" To make certain the soldier took his spear and rammed it up under the ribs up through Yeshua's diaphragm and into His heart.

John says,

But when they came to Jesus and found that he was already dead, they did not break his legs. Instead, one of the soldiers pierced Jesus' side [Greek, pleuran] with a spear, bringing a sudden flow of blood and water. The man who saw it has given testimony, and his testimony is true. He knows that he tells the truth, and he testifies so that you also may believe.

- John 19:33-36

Some have suggested a medical explanation for the flow of blood and water but I don't see a sluggish draining of blood and a bit of watery fluid as constituting "a sudden flow." First there was a flow of blood and second, a flow of water. I think that Mel Gibson got this scene right in The Passion of the Christ as he shows a gush of water coming from Jesus' side.

Here is a principle. There is no flow of water without a flow of blood. The waters of the Holy Spirit don't flow without an acknowledgement of His sacrificial blood. This is why all heaven gratefully sings the praise of the Lamb!

INTRODUCING THE LION/LAMB

Revelation five begins with heaven confounded. A book must be opened. It is no ordinary book. It is the book of life! If the book is not opened God's redemptive story will not unfold. But there is no one in the universe worthy to remove the seven seals and open the book. John is so moved that he goes into deep weeping.

He is comforted by one of heaven's elders, "Do not

weep! See, the Lion of the tribe of Judah, the Root of David, has triumphed. He is able to open the scroll and its seven seals." When John turns to look at this Lion He discovers rather, a Lamb. Join the worship as the Lamb is gloriously introduced!

¹Then I saw in the right hand of him who sat on the throne a scroll with writing on both sides and sealed with seven seals. ²And I saw a mighty angel proclaiming in a loud voice, "Who is worthy to break the seals and open the scroll?" ³But no one in heaven or on earth or under the earth could open the scroll or even look inside it. ⁴I wept and wept because no one was found who was worthy to open the scroll or look inside. ⁵Then one of the elders said to me, "Do not weep! See, the Lion of the tribe of Judah, the Root of David, has triumphed. He is able to open the scroll and its seven seals." ⁶Then I saw a Lamb, looking as if it had been slain, standing in the center of the throne, encircled by the four living creatures and the elders. He had seven horns and seven eyes, which are the seven spirits of God sent out into all the earth. ⁷He came and took the scroll from the right hand of him who sat on the throne. 8 And when he had taken it, the four living creatures and the twenty-four elders fell down before the Lamb. Each one had a harp and they were holding golden bowls full of incense, which are the prayers of the saints. ⁹And they sang a new song:

"You are worthy to take the scroll and to open its seals, because you were slain, and with your blood you purchased men for God from every tribe and language and

*people and nation. ¹⁰You have made them
to be a kingdom and priests to serve our
God, and they will reign on the earth."*

*¹¹Then I looked and heard the voice of many an-
gels, numbering thousands upon thousands, and
ten thousand times ten thousand. They encircled
the throne and the living creatures and the elders.
¹²In a loud voice they sang:*

*"Worthy is the Lamb, who was slain, to
receive power and wealth and wisdom and
strength and honor and glory and praise!"*

*¹³Then I heard every creature in heaven and on
earth and under the earth and on the sea, and all
that is in them, singing:*

*"To him who sits on the throne and to the
Lamb be praise and honor and glory and
power, for ever and ever!"*

*¹⁴The four living creatures said, "Amen,"
and the elders fell down and worshiped.*
- Revelation 5:1-14

What climactic worship! Don't you wish to stick close
to the Lamb, our magnificent escort!

As John had this heavenly vision I suspect he harkened
back to the Jordan River decades before. As a young
man he had been a disciple of John the Baptist. The
Baptist pointed out Jesus saying, "Behold, the Lamb of
God who takes away the sins of the world." John tre-
mendously loved and esteemed his Lord as they traveled about Galilee, but this trip to heaven presented his
Master as exponentially glorious! How could young

John have anticipated such a ravishing revelation of the Baptist's words?

Our Lord is revealed in many forms in the Gospels. He is Rabbi, Savior, Redeemer, Son of Man, Physician, Friend - and the list goes on. In Revelation Jesus is the bright morning Star! He is the brilliant King, Lord and judge. He is the mighty warrior leading heaven's cavalry. The predominant picture of Jesus is of a Lamb. Thirty times in Revelation Jesus is referenced as The Lamb!

He, with His Father, sits on the throne and is the object of heaven's worship. Heaven's music is written for Him. Heaven's voices rumble His praise! He alone has the virtue and authority to open the Book of Life. His followers overcome the world with the Lamb's blood. The Lamb is a Bridegroom. With His Father they illuminate the world so there is no need for the sun! All of heaven's amazing creatures, the angels and redeemed give adoring focus to the Lamb.

YESHUA IS STILL LIFTING HIS VOICE!

Jesus stood and shouted to the people crowded into the temple complex, "If anyone is thirsty, let him come to me and drink. Whoever believes in me, as the Scripture has said, streams of living water will flow from within him."

John heard the same invitation shouted out in heaven.

It is done! I am the Alpha and the Omega, the Beginning and the End. I will give of the fountain of the water of life freely to him who thirsts.
                                        - Revelation 21:6

Whoever is thirsty, let him come; and whoever wishes, let him take the free gift of the water of life.
— Revelation 22:17

Remember once again, the One who said, "I am thirsty" on the cross is the source of living water? Moses struck the rock and water poured out of it to the thirsty desert wanderers? That rock was Christ. His wounding and brokenness brought forth a river. (Exodus 17:6). Without a flow of blood there could never be a flow of living water.

We usually think of clothing being stained by blood, not whitened. But we read in Revelation 7:14, "These are they who have come out of the great tribulation; they have washed their robes and made them white in the blood of the Lamb." His beautiful, ruby-red blood makes us white as snow!

> *"See, from His head, His hands, His feet*
> *Sorrow and love flow mingled down*
> *Did e'er such love and sorrow meet*
> *Or thorns compose so rich a crown?"*

The day of His passion makes possible a day of mercy.

> *On that day a fountain will be opened to the house of David and the inhabitants of Jerusalem, to cleanse them from sin and impurity."*
> — Zechariah 13:1

How can we help but be grateful to the Lamb, or yield Him our total devotion? He is our Gusher, our Gully Washer, and The Faithful Fountain. Out of Him flows all we long for - boldness, power, grace, wisdom, insight, judgment, mercy and love!

YOUR FAITH PRIMES THE PUMP!

Happy birthday! A nicely wrapped package, with your name, sits before you on the table. You expect a nice surprise. You order your favorite meal on the menu and expectantly wait, your eyes towards the kitchen door. Expectation and faith go together. If we are missing expectation perhaps there is not much faith.

Some say they believe in Christ's return, but they lack eager anticipation. Some say they believe in the doctrine of the Holy Spirit but have little expectation that this afternoon the Spirit will surge through their minds and hearts directing new courses of action.

I coach myself to be eagerly expectant; "Jesus said if I believe in Him (and I do) I will have His river flow in me. I actively believe in Him this moment! I expect streams to flow now! Here they come!"

There are plenty of promises connected to believing. The one we latch onto is John 7:38:

Whoever believes in me, as the Scripture has said, streams of living water will flow from within him.

The Apostle Paul reminds us that faith primes the pump.

Did you receive the Spirit by observing the law, or by believing what you heard?
- Galatians 3:2

Does God give you His Spirit and work miracles among you because you observe the law, or because you believed what you heard?

— Galatians 3:5

That we might receive the promise of the Spirit through faith.

— Galatians 3:14

It is good to be good. This is expected of us. But the Holy Spirit is not given us because we are good, but because we believe in His goodness!

When we ask for the Spirit's help, comfort, power, love or insight we do so expectantly! We eagerly expect him to keep His promise,

"I will pour water upon him that is thirsty, and floods upon the dry ground.

— Isaiah 44:3

Here is where it would be helpful to have friends with experience in the river to pray personally for you. We do this at the Riverfront Property Seminar.

In Acts 9:17,

Ananias went to the house and entered it. Placing his hands on Saul, he said, "Brother Saul, the Lord-Jesus, who appeared to you on the road as you were coming here-has sent me so that you may see again and be filled with the Holy Spirit.

There are many times in scripture where the power of the Spirit is conferred by laying on hands. It is so helpful to have a point of contact with empowered believers.

It is like getting jumper cables to a dead battery.

REPENTANCE AND REFRESHING

One expression of faith is repentance. Shortly after Pentecost Peter preached,

Repent, then, and turn to God, so that your sins may be wiped out, that times of refreshing may come from the Lord.

- Acts 3:19-20

Repenting means changing your mind. If you are driving to go to dinner at a Chinese restaurant and part way see a sign for a new Mexican restaurant, and decide to go there instead, you went through a process of repentance. You rethought your plans and made a different decision.

Peter uses the expression "refreshing" to refer to the Spirit's ministry. When we turn from sin and turn to God our sins are wiped out and we have a welcome to the river. Convert this truth to action:

- Turn from sin!
- Turn to God!
- Have your sins wiped out!
- Be refreshed by the Spirit!

We may repent of lies, pride and sexual sin, of worry, gossip and theft. And we should! But here is the Great Sin, according to Jeremiah 2:13—independent self-sufficiency.

For my people have committed two evils; they have forsaken me the fountain of living waters, and hewed them out cisterns, broken cisterns, that can hold no water."

Again, the prophet defines the great sin of living independent of God in Jeremiah 17:13,

> *They have forsaken the LORD, the fountain of living waters.*

Option one, stagnant leaking cisterns or option two, a fresh flowing fountain. When we consider the options, we will eagerly give up our leaky cisterns for the Lord, and His living waters! Put your heart and body in a humble posture and pray this simple prayer.

> *Dear Lord,*
> *I have presumed that I can live independently.*
> *I have tried to store up things to satisfy, but they leak out through the cracks.*
> *I see how foolish I have been!*
> *Your offer of living water is too good to pass by.*
> *I turn to You! Please, wash away my sins.*
> *Lamb of God, let me walk forever with you!*
> *Quench my thirst and lead me by the riverside.*

Now my Friend, be still and watch expectantly as the Lord responds!

Here is where it would be good to be free of preconceptions of what the Holy Spirit should feel like or do. You may sense something quickly or there may be some waiting. You may feel a powerful Surge, but don't miss Ankle Deep Trickling!

We wait a handful of minutes for fast food. How long will we wait on God? One hundred twenty waited in an upper room for 10 days. Be patient, expectant and still. As you wait do a personal assessment. Do you have sensations in your body? What thoughts are in your mind? How are you feeling emotionally?

Your only job is to trust His kind intentions and be in receiving mode! Remember - patient and eager expectation!

You might want to get a pen and journal your thoughts and feelings. Be aware. What are you sensing? Is that love, joy and peace you are feeling? Yes, you are in the river and the water is flowing!

Deep calls to deep in the roar of your waterfalls.
- Psalm 42:7

Now would be a good time to fold the book and soak in His loving-kindness! Let the river flow!

**Follow the Lamb
And He will lead you to the Waters of Life.**

For the Lamb at the center of the throne will be their shepherd; He will lead them to springs of living water. And God will wipe away every tear from their eyes.
- Revelation 7:17

Episode 4 :

PIPES AND WIRES

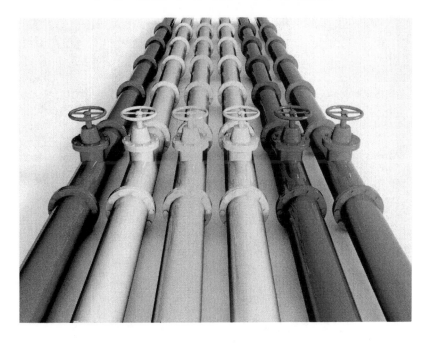

SKIP IT

One of my early memories is being at a river and dad showing us kids how to skip rocks. I watched amazed as dad defied the laws of nature, flinging flat stones. They hopped, bounced and slid, inscribing fascinating circles and swirls on the face of the deep.

First attempts produced only splashes but with adjustments came the ever-so-satisfying skip! There were shouts of commentary following our hopping, skipping, sliding missiles.

Skipping stones is a true mark of manhood. If a man has found a woman who skips stones he has found a rare treasure! If you have not learned how there is still hope. Check into a clinic where you may get remedial help.

Jesus and his disciples practiced this manly art at Galilee. Bible scholars have pretty well proven Philip had the longest throw but Matthew had the knack for getting the most skips.

Stone skipping goes on the resume. If you really want to impress people at the job interview bring up skipping! Remember, be confident but not arrogant.

Perhaps there are more profound things to start with, but for now, let's skip it.

THE PROBLEM OF SUPER HEROES

Perhaps 700 people were there. A well-known minister brought an inspirational message. A couple hundred came forward. He shared prophetic words. He had a wonderful healing gift. Members of the crowd deeply appreciated his anointing. But I left frustrated!

It was one more meeting where hundreds of people seeking ministry waited on a single individual to do the job. There were dozens if not hundreds of capable ministers in the audience but for several hours only one was engaged. This is not the way God designed ministry to be done. I was exasperated, because you were not there, ministering beside the guest powerhouse!

Josheb-Basshebeth, a Tahkemonite, was chief of the Three; he raised his spear against eight hundred men, whom he killed in one encounter.
                                    - 2 Samuel 23:8

We love stories where standalone heroes like Samson slay a thousand or a young David takes down a giant.

I am in favor of spiritual superheroes, yet I would rather see a thousand saints energized and active than a single superstar doing it all. God typically calls armies to win wars, not single fantastic gladiators. I look for a day when we all will be engaged!

PLUMBING COLLEGE

I dreamed I was walking through a college library where dozens of students sat diligently studying the art of plumbing. In front of the students' cubicles were posted technical plumbing diagrams. One student came to me and spoke earnestly, "I just want to go someplace where they need the most basic of plumbing." It seemed that he had a broken heart for those who were thirsty. As he spoke I imagined a poor village where they might walk miles to get water. How they would love a simple spigot of water in their town square.

ELECTRICAL COLLEGE

In another dream I was visiting a college as a guest speaker. I had brought in a very thick electrical power cable. One end was tied into a power panel, the other was lying on the ground and not yet hooked up to anything. I felt the power cable would activate the students.

GETTING AN EDUCATION

Would you like a bit of schooling in the plumbing and electrical arts? Having remodeled a couple homes and owned apartment buildings I have firsthand experience in plumbing and wiring. I won't traumatize you with stories of running to the store four times to get a water heater installed, or welding screwdrivers with electrical sparks. Spurts and jolts have been part of my education. What kind of education have you had?

I'm not sure I would read a book on how to fly an airplane, and go straight out to try. Tutoring and hands on training might be helpful. I encourage you to find spiritual mentors with plumbing and electrical experience. Do lab work for "More is caught than taught."

Yeshua's disciples had fabulous mentoring. They observed Jesus heal the sick and cast out demons. Reading between the lines, it looks like they practiced under their Rabbi's supervision. He sent out the twelve, two by two, to "do the stuff." They were frontrunners, giving people a taste of the kingdom and a heads up, saying in essence, "We are here to let you know the kingdom is at hand! Jesus is making a circuit of cities and coming to your town!"

The disciples were given these instructions.

As you go, preach this message: 'The kingdom

of heaven is near.' Heal the sick, raise the dead, cleanse those who have leprosy, drive out demons. Freely you have received, freely give.
- Matthew 10:7-9

WATER THROUGH THE PIPES

I was sitting in my office when a woman came to talk to my secretary. I spoke through the open door, "Claudine, how are you?" She answered, "Fine, but arthritis in my thumbs is bothering me." I felt the Spirit and said, "Come over here. " She walked to my chair and I put my hands over her thumbs. I prayed a simple prayer. I felt the Spirit rise up through my waist and like water flow down my arms. Power flowed through my hands. She was cured.

IT WAS ELECTRIC

My back was tense and tired. My nerves were pinched. This was a serious, long-term back ache. My friend Jean put her hands on my back and prayed! The power was electric! My chest pumped up and a rod of steel ran down my backbone. I felt like Popeye after his spinach! Jean was a cable for God's electricity!

If several of us held hands and the people at either end held the hot and ground wire we would all get a tingle. Ministry to others is as simple as holding Jesus' hand on one side and your friend's on the other. Power is conducted by contact.

There is satisfaction in being a channel of the Father's

love, power, and wisdom. I want you to have that satisfaction! I want you journaling about it and modeling your practice to others.

BE CAREFUL IN THE BATHTUB WITH ELECTRICITY!

Yeshua gave a wonderful depiction of the flow of life in John 15:5:

> *I am the vine; you are the branches. If a man remains in me and I in him, he will bear much fruit; apart from me you can do nothing.*

He addressed an agrarian society where everyone grew grapes for food and drink, and as trellises in place of air conditioning.

We "gather" grapes at the store. Some have no idea what a grapevine vine looks like. Jesus today would choose an image we understand. He might say, ""I am the power outlet and my Father is the utility company. When you are plugged into me you will live powerfully. Unless you are plugged into the "juice" you will go dead.

When we screw in a light bulb and power is switched on the bulb "puts a demand" on the system. There is nothing arrogant in the light bulb's request; it is simply expectant of a distribution of power.

The electrician speaks water language - flow, current, surge and circuit. The surge of God's electricity reveals our identity.

MAKING CONNECTIONS

The smell of fresh paint is still in the air. Several boxes of new appliances have been bought to outfit the kitchen. They sit on the counter. Perhaps Disney could help us with this scene. Imagine a muffled excitement within those boxes, and voices when the lids came off.

"I'm so excited! I'm going to be a kitchen appliance!"
"Me too, me too! What are you?"
"I don't know. What are you?"
"I don't know. But I am about to find out!"

How will an appliance learn its identity and function? By being plugged in! The flow of electricity will reveal the blender, coffee pot and food processor. Appliances activated by power learn about themselves.

When power gets to a toaster it toasts, when it goes through a microwave it excites electrons, when it flows through a light bulb it glows. When the current gets to a prophet it activates prophecy, when it gets to righteous person it activates righteous works. When the current electrifies the singer or social activist, the teacher or artist - beautiful things are energized. Can you imagine kitchen appliances arguing over what is the true manifestation of electricity? How silly!

When we move in the power of God's Spirit we discover things like purpose, function and direction. We discover joy, sometimes with trembling as we feel His righteousness judgments!

How are we defined? By making connection! Jesus

might say, "Unless you are plugged into me you will never saw, drill, wash, circulate or calculate. But if you are plugged in you are going to discover delight and significance, finding satisfaction in your purpose and design."

Many languish without a sense of purpose. They have never felt the energizing current. You can change that! You can be the extension cord to activate them! You can be the jumper cables to get them running!

CONDUCTIVITY

I played with a fork at the power plug and gained an education every child should possess, a lesson about conductivity! When a circuit is bridged by contact electricity gets exciting! Given enough voltage and proximity electricity will actually leap through space, arcing from one object to another. Do your kids know about this?

Heaven arced down on Pentecost and later on Cornelius' household. No human being was touching the people. The Spirit simply jumped the gap and electrified believing hearts. There are times in a worship service where the power of God may jump the gap. Those who are not personally prayed for feel the jolt and receive healing, deliverance, visions, and any number of blessings.

COMMUNICATING WITH TOUCH

The book of Acts has accounts where laying on hands created a point of contact, and power flowed.

Then Peter and John placed their hands on them, and they received the Holy Spirit.

- Acts 8:17

Paul went in to see him and, after prayer, placed his hands on him and healed him.

- Acts 28:8

Do not neglect your gift, which was given you through a prophetic message when the body of elders laid their hands on you.

- 1 Timothy 4:14

We may feel the power of God when no one is near us. This is arching. We may also experience His power as friends pray and touch us. This is conductivity.

GET A GRIP!

We write a Blog at *www.landingstripenterprises.com*. Please come and join us! Here is a piece that seems to fit.

The woman with the issue of blood came up and grabbed Jesus' prayer shawl as He walked through a crushing crowd. She was healed as she laid hold of Him! (Mark 5:25-34).

So many sit at home longing that Jesus would knock on the door and say, "Hi, I'm here to meet your needs! What have you got?" This woman did not wait in passivity for Jesus to come by and touch her. She sought Him out and grabbed Him!

When a curling iron is switched on a "demand" is put on the power company. When we deliberately plug into Jesus, we are not arrogantly "demanding" but expectantly anticipating!

We use the expression, "Get a grip." We find it illustrated in scripture. Samson got a grip on a donkey's jaw bone. Jael seized the hammer and tent peg. Eleazar gripped his sword. When the battle was done His fingers needed to be pried off.

Wouldn't it be nice to have wisdom? Get a grip! Wouldn't it be helpful to have provision? Get a grip! Wouldn't it be great to have deliverance and healing? Get a grip on the Savior!

Was Jesus ticked off at the woman for touching Him? He might have shamed her; "Why have you contaminated me by touching me?" Instead, He blessed her for her faith. She laid hold of Jesus and got what she sought!

Anemic, passive, hope says, "Wouldn't it be nice…." A gripping faith says," I must and will connect with Jesus. I am going to find him and hold Him!" Jacob said to his wrestling Partner. "I will not let go of you until you bless me!"

Isaiah tells of a sinful nation that had no more gumption to seek God.

> *No one calls on your name or strives to lay hold of you.*
>
> - Isaiah 64:7

Contrast Matthew, who shows a people with resolve.

From the days of John the Baptist until now, the kingdom of heaven has been forcefully advancing, and forceful men lay hold of it.
                              - Matthew 11:12

We need to be fierce, vigorous, and perhaps belligerent, to latch onto the kingdom! We press to lay hold of the One who throbs with Life! He may be invisible but He is not insubstantial! Clutch the door frame or kitchen table and tell God, "Just like I am holding on to this I am holding on to You, for Dear Life!

Do you have one of those pathetic, flaccid handshakes? It's time to exercise your squeeze until you have a vice grip, bulldog clasp on the One Who has what you need. Latch on aggressively to the willingness of God!

I held him and would not let him go...
                              - Song of Solomon 3:4

I am curious. Do you sense a flow of the river?

HUMBLE GRATITUDE

Do you think a pipe should boast about transporting water, or a wire brag about conducting energy? God is the source so He gets the glory! We take pleasure and gratification in being used! God is glorified for making the fruit tree but the tree celebrates while being fruitful!

It is dangerous to compare yourself with others. What happens when the apple compares itself to the orange, the prophet to the pastor, or the scholar to the warrior?

If we seem more capable or proficient we may falsely elevate ourselves, taking on an attitude of superiority. If we seem to underperform, we can't do what they do, we plummet into self-depreciation and inferiority.

It can be a heady thing to be used by God. Don't let pride bite you! We may mistakenly assume that the Lamb is using us because we are spiritually superior. This is not true. It is simply His power and love linked with our availability.

Rejoice when you brothers and sisters are used by God. Celebrate! People are helped and the Father is glorified!

CONCEITED AND INSECURE APPLIANCES

Can you imagine appliances arguing over who is the greatest, or worrying that their lives don't count?

"I can capture pictures."
"Sure, but I condense moisture from the air."
"I can sound a fire alarm."
"Big deal. I can pump water."
"I know the time."
"That's nothing. I guide airplanes!"

Other appliances are down in the mouth, doubtful of their worth.

"I'm not important like the water heater."
"I'm next to worthless. All I do is sharpen pencils."
"I'm a loser. Everyone is grossed out when they learn I'm a garbage disposal. I wish I was a cat scan!"

Our significance is not just in function, but in relationship. At the auction house my alarm clock might sell for 50 cents, but the celebrity's for $500. A servant of the king may take more satisfaction than the servant of the tinsmith.

We are born with pre-loaded value, installed by our Creator. He made us for His own glory and pleasure. How delightful to consider, we bring Him pleasure!

MY FAVORITE THING!

I love when "God shows up" in the rumble of worshipful praise among thousands. But my all-time favorite corporate experiences are in small groups! I love to see saints engaged, encouraging one another!
Someone shares a concern and "one-anothering" begins!

One prays;
Another shares a scripture.
There are words of encouragement.
Another has a perfect fit testimony.
One or two have prophecies,
A healing gift shows up,
A spontaneous song sings out.
Another has a connecting dream and interpretation.
Someone shares a $50 bill.
Another says, "My boss wants to hire someone just like you!"

The person who receives ministry leaves thoroughly fortified! The whole group of friends is glad to be used! It simply can't be beat! May groups like this multiply where the Lamb is worshipped at the riverside and godly character is pursued in loving community. The early church tasted this supernatural fellowship. Take for example 1 Corinthians 14:24-25:

> *But if an unbeliever or someone who does not understand comes in while everybody is prophesying, he will be convinced by all that he is a sinner and will be judged by all, and the secrets of his heart will be laid bare. So he will fall down and worship God, exclaiming, "God is really among you!"*

An unbelieving man sits at the kitchen table with chatty saints. They celebrate the latest answers to prayer and evidences of the Father's goodness. Two guys at the table get supernatural words of knowledge. They tell the man what he said out loud to himself while shaving that morning! God is "reading the mail." The man is listening!

How often do you act as a conduit of God's grace? Often? Once in a while? Perhaps you just want to get started. Here is where the books and advice could become endless. Let's do our best to keep things simple.

We lived in a country home with plenty of water. A spring up the mountain poured into a pipe. We were down the hill with plenty of water pressure. The process of being a minister is rather simple. Run your pipes to God's heaven then stay low so the water may gain pressure. Finally, be prepared to love people.

BECOMING PRACTITIONERS

Doctors practice medicine. We get queasy when they practice on us. Don't judge them harshly; we also develop ministry skills by practice. Seek to bless and not harm. Do not be in such a hurry to help that you are insensitive to your friend's thoughts and feelings.

Talk up Jesus!

> ...*Worship God! For the testimony of Jesus is the spirit of prophecy.*
>
> - Revelation 19:10

Here is a principle. Keep Jesus central in your worship and conversation, for when you talk up Jesus the Spirit empowers prophecy. Talking up the glories of the Lamb stirs up spiritual gifts in general. Share how powerful, loving, faithful, gracious, beautiful, redemptive, just and compassionate our Redeemer is. If you lead people to the Lamb they will find the river, because He walks beside it.

Ministering in teams increases perspective, thoroughness and effectiveness. Practice waiting and listening in small groups.

Gather God's love and compassion. Value people highly! Consider the person before you as the most important person on the planet.

Ministering is a privilege. Do not regard yourself as a superior ministering to an inferior. Come as a friend.

Put more confidence in God's ability to use you than in

your limited capabilities.

Ask permission. "May I pray for you?" "May I put my hand on your shoulder?" "People have every right to refuse you. But when they welcome you they welcome the Spirit.

Don't pin people into a corner. Invite them into open places. This gives you and the person you are sharing with a safe place to learn the ways of the Spirit.

Ask, don't tell. "I am feeling peace. Do you feel that?"

Rather than say, "Thus sayeth the Lord!" you might say, "I feel strongly the Lord is saying this, or ministering that. Does that register or ring with you?"

Avoid duplicating your last approach with a new person. God is creative and customizes ministry according to the uniqueness of individuals.

Be still and quiet. You are not in a hurry. You are not waiting for your good idea or feeling but for God.

PRAYERS YOU MAY PRAY

The Holy Spirit did not fall on Pentecost because a prayer was precisely articulated. The disciples caught the down-pour simply because they believed their risen Lord. He told them to wait, and they did! We can speculate as to their prayers but their posture of anticipation is what counted.

Keep prayers simple and to the point. Heaven is not responding to remarkable prayers but believing hearts.

Our Father is deserving of thanks, and so praise-worthy! Here is a good place to start! The river flows out of a house of prayer and worship! Is that you?

Pray with hope and expectancy. Pray according to the authority vested in Jesus.

You may have the receiver make "I believe" statements.

"I believe:
> You are here!
> You are compassionate!
> You have power to rescue!
> You are generous!
> You answer prayer!
> You want to fill me!
> You wish to give me gifts!"

Sometimes I will remind the receiver of Jesus' words,

If anyone is thirsty, let him come to me and drink. Whoever believes in me, as the Scripture has said, streams of living water will flow from within him.
- John 7:37-38

They may pray, "Lord Jesus, I am thirsty. I come to You to drink. I believe in You. Let streams of living water flow from within me."

Thank Jesus for the promise of the Spirit. The believer should not be shy. We yield all to Him. He in turn shares all with us!

If sins come to your friend's mind guide them in confession and receiving forgiveness. "Forgive me for forsaking the Fountain of life and for minimizing my need for you. Wash away the contamination, the sin, the pain and the sorrow!"

Again, keep your prayers simple. "Let your river flow through me. Make me aware of Your love. Refresh me!"

LISTEN AND WAIT

My friend John was ministering in a church and invited people to come forward. About 15 people stood in a circle. John prayed a short prayer for the Holy Spirit to move among us. I had no sense of the Spirit's presence. I think others felt the same. John stood patiently and waited. I was amazed that he waited several minutes and nothing seemed to be happening.

I might have said, "Well, God bless you all, have a good night." John continued to patiently wait. After several minutes one of the men suddenly fell to the hard concrete floor! He was overcome. A deep, deep work was going on! He was being freed from addictions and receiving healing. Others were also touched. If John had not been willing to lead us in waiting we might have missed our opportunity.

Waiting and listening is our job. Power and love is the Spirit's

SENSES AND FEELINGS, THOUGHTS AND IMPRESSIONS

If you feel peace, speak it to your friend. If you feel holiness, communicate it. If you feel love or strength or caution or compassion, convert those feelings into spoken blessings or prayers. What are you feeling that you can impart?

Thoughts and impressions can also be converted into blessings and prayers. What are the thoughts and pictures in your mind? Why do you suppose the Spirit has put them there?

Many times I have prayed for others and felt a pumping action in my torso. I stand and wait a bit. I feel a trickling filling my body cavity like the down-stroke of a well pump. When I sense the waters have filled the pump I pray and feel the upstroke. Waters rise through my waist, go down my arms and through my hands to refresh my brother or sister.

Many are unaware of impressions within them. I may be in a group and ask the members what they are sensing. They are quiet. One or two say," I don't sense anything." Then I might share, for example, "I've been seeing a monarch butterfly." Two or three may then respond, "Actually, I was thinking of butterflies as well!" Although it was in their consciousness it was on the edges and out of focus. When we are alert we find God speaking to us through complementary impressions.

Keep in mind that the Holy Spirit activates each of us uniquely. I am intrigued with the diverse ways the Spirit pours through believers. Differing gifting and personalities make team ministry look like a laser light show in fountain jets!

BREAKOUT SESSIONS

In the Riverfront Property Seminar we would do break-out sessions here. You would be in a small group with other young practitioners, and overseen by trusted leaders. You would each have the opportunity to minister and receive ministry. And when it was done you would have things to write in your journal!

You can put together ministry groups in your context. Round up young aspiring plumbers and electricians, humble and willing to learn. If possible, find those experienced in these arts to provide modeling and oversight. Wait on the Lord, listen to His voice and then be conduits of the Spirit's electrified water. And yes, keep your journal handy. God loves to reveal Himself to those who seek Him!

Don't be biased in the way you think the Spirit should move. At times the waters whisper and at times the waters roar! Stick close to the Lamb! He will guide you where you need to be.

Remember to communicate with one another in the process. "What are you thinking, feeling, sensing?" You do not have to force anything. The work is of God. Simply do your best to keep your pipes clean and your wires shiny.

**Follow the Lamb
And He will lead you to the Waters of life.**

For the Lamb at the center of the throne will be their shepherd; He will lead them to springs of living water. And God will wipe away every tear from their eyes.

- Revelation 7:17

Episode 5 :

DIGGING WELLS AND REMOVING CAPS

OUR NOBLE WELL-DIGGING PATRIARCHS

The Patriarchs Abraham, Isaac and Jacob were regarded as honorable for many reasons. One is, they dug wells to provided water for their clans. Noble minded people dig wells, water works which satisfy needs.

There are intense conflicts and grumbling over water rights. The Patriarchs came up with honorable solutions for the clashes and complaints. Most involved time consuming, back-breaking labor. Answers to problems came with shovels attached!

What do we do when we discover our river bottom has dried into cracked puzzle pieces? Grab a spade!

RESPONDING TO THIRST

Thirsty people grumble, naturally. Churches are not happy with water shortages. We moan and complain. "Where is God's presence?" "This church is bone dry!" "Where did the love and power go?" "Someone drained the pool!"

Some of us church hop looking for a place with dancing fountains. We hope for an easy drink. Others join a community, and when they realize water is needed, they do all they can to see their tribe gets it. Some complain, or leave. Others dig.

Responsible believers take ownership of problems and work on solutions.

Sometimes responding to the Spirit is a cinch. We cannon-ball in, swim and frolic! When rivers go dry people dig wells. They think this is preferable to dying. If the river goes arid don't despair, get to work! You remember Jesus saying, "He who believes in me, out of his inner being will flow…." The work of faith produces flow. Digging wells is also done by faith.

I visited southern Israel near Beer Sheva, the well of the oath, and saw a hand dug well. I could tell it was deep because the pebble I dropped took a long time before it plopped. It must have been hard work. If you live in a place with a handful of inches of rain a year you dig or die. Don't whine if you don't sense the presence of God. Get digging! Dig deep via hope and humility and intercession and gain water for your clan.

Do you want to see a party? Dig a well in a barren place where people walk miles for water. We were part of a well drilling project in Kenya. What a party they had when the water started pumping!

Many churches do not feel like partying. Who wants a dehydrated fellowship? Some dread going to worship service, fearing the next one will be as dry as the last.

Our neighbors and people in faraway places are waiting for us to confirm that Jesus makes good His promise of living water. They try drugs, entertainments and wacked out philosophies to satisfy their thirst. They despair that real drink can be found. You have their answer, but it may require digging.

THE WELL AT BEER

During the wanderings of Israel they dug a well. We get a snatch of the story in Numbers 21:16-18.

From there they continued on to Beer, the well where the LORD said to Moses, 'Gather the people together and I will give them water.

Then Israel sang this song:

Spring up, O well!
Sing about it,

about the well that the princes dug,
that the nobles of the people sank—
the nobles with scepters and staffs.

THE MARK OF NOBILITY

Those that accessed water for the community were not commoners, they were nobles! Many want a noble title – Duke or Duchess, Apostle, Evangelist or Pastor. Don't expect people to think you noble because of your genealogy. It will come because of you noble lifestyle, the way you care for others.

Noble leaders realize their responsibility for providing water. They do not idly show up for church, turn on the tap and expect anointed ministry. They probe God. They augur into His heart. They burrow into his word. These leaders are to be honored!

Digging wells is the work of genuine monarchs, knights, barons and counts. They willingly get their hands dirtied and blistered, down in the gloom, for the sake of their people. Laboring in a murky well- shaft may not be your idea of fun but it is a great idea for survival.

Nobility is gained by noble deeds. It is an expression of character. When water is found we celebrate, and the diggers are esteemed!

CELEBRATING

Water in short supply occasions quarrels and contentions. Neighbors fight. When there is abundance fearful apprehension is washed away. We are friends again!

If you delve into the earth boring into the unseen depths you might stumble on diamonds, emeralds and rubies. You might discover natural gas, oil and coal, perhaps ancient fossils. You might also discover water. And if you, your family and flocks were really thirsty you would bring them together, drink deep and throw a party!

Those about you are watching you dig. They hope for your success because they would love a big draught of water. In fact, they would take a water break and throw a party!

JACOB GETS THE LID OFF

Jacob fled for his life. His brother literally wanted to kill him! He came to the distant land of Padan Aram where shepherd girls were waiting to water their congregation. These shepherdesses were delayed because those strong enough to remove the stone protecting the well had not arrived. When Jacob saw Rachel daughter of Laban, his mother's brother, he manhandled the stone from the mouth of the well and watered the sheep.

Several people were needed to move the stone but Jacob single-handedly removed it. Jacob was tough, the kind of guy who wrestles angels. By the way, he later married Rachel who was probably swooning, "My, he is so strong and handsome!"

GETTING THE CAP OFF

Many believers have perfectly fine wells with lots of water but their wells are capped. They cannot access the water because heavy weights block the opening. Those caps may seem so immense; it appears a herculean task to remove them. We can help one another get the caps off!

If you or your friend feels a restriction in experiencing the Father's love and power see if one of these caps need to be removed.

- Unbelief—God is not interested in me.
- Fear—I dread the future
- Pride—I must look important
- Presumption—I can do it my way
- Hard heartedness—Being vulnerable with God is for the weak
- Grief—Nothing can remove this pain
- Unforgiveness—I would rather have them punished than personally know God's peace

Ask God for discernment. He may reveal blockages like apathy, self-sufficiency, false loves or distractions. He will show you how to remove the blockages and access the water. Remember, God's plan to get the lids off may involve other brothers and sisters.

PERSPECTIVE ON EASE AND HARD LABOR

We are grateful for times were accessing water is a breeze. This is the grace of God. There are other times where we need to dig, and the labors are difficult. This is also the grace of God! Look for the Lamb beside you in the well-shaft!

Out of a river, or out of a well, we access waters by faith.

Whether it comes easy or with toil, we trust in God's generous provision. There are times we must dig. May it prove our nobility!

A GREAT BRIDGE!

In May of 1995 I had a dream that would get on my top 10. I suddenly found myself standing on a gangway one hundred feet over a large suspension bridge. The bridge was six lanes wide. No cars were on the bridge but a group of about 8 people were in the middle, standing in a circle of prayer.

Interestingly, the bridge ran right down the middle of an immense river! As I looked, a wave lapped over the deck of the bridge covering the people praying below. I was alarmed, thinking they were washed off the bridge, but they were all there after the water rolled away. I ran down stairs to check on the people and when I got to the bottom I came to a large room where dozens of people were praying.

I believe the last-days Church will not bridge from one spiritual awakening to another. As we become the house of prayer we will endlessly experience the river of life.

SCANNING THE WATERFRONT

Our Inheritance in Messiah is a stretch of Riverfront Property! It is a delightful place of connection – connection with the Lamb and with His people!

I would love to go fishing with you at the Dead Sea. It may be renamed The Lively Sea. Are you anxious to sample the fruit there? The most delicious thing will be to walk with the Lamb!

Today is yesterday's future. Since you live in the future make the most of it. Make following the Lamb your daily habit. As you trust Him more you will experience more of the inner river.

May you draw from the river with ease! If you must dig wells, be of good cheer. Dirt under your nails means water for your tribe. You do a noble work!

Many have yet to learn that Jesus is "the Lamb of God who takes away the sins of the world." Not only are non-believers in fatal dehydration but millions who acknowledge Messiah live with a dribble when they might have a river!

Your neighbors and those at the edges of the world thirst for what you have. They desire an authentic demonstration of love, power, truth and righteousness. They are waiting for you, God's delivery system!

May water flow from your buckets. May your seed have abundant water!

Follow the Lamb and He will lead you to the Waters of life.

For the Lamb at the center of the throne will be their shepherd; He will lead them to springs of living water. And God will wipe away every tear from their eyes.

- Revelation 7:17

Addendum 1:

DREAMS AND VISIONS

If you asked Joel what the outpouring of the Holy Spirit looked like he would answer, "Dreams, Visions and Prophecy."

> *I will pour out my Spirit on all people.*
> *Your sons and daughters will prophesy,*
> *your old men will dream dreams,*
> *your young men will see visions.*
> — Joel 2:28

One night my wife and daughter, Theresa, both had dreams about synchronized swimming. There was nothing going on in our world that would make us think of this, God was simply communicating how fun and beautiful it is when we synchronize our movements in the Holy Spirit

In a dream I was registering to go to a college and began to point to people around me saying, "Look at all the Tennesseans!" There were over a dozen dreams about being in Tennessee. They were part of our decision to move there.

We have often received chastening and correction, confirmation and guidance through dreams. We have been warned so that we might pray and be aware. We receive wisdom through these provisions.

It was about two in the afternoon and I was tired. I flopped down on the bed to rest. Instantly I saw a vision of a cowboy wearing leather and covered with silver conchos. We had been wondering if we should join a local cowboy church. The vision helped us make our decision.

Joel prophesied a rainstorm of dreams and visions. I anticipate a deluge. Record your dreams and visions. Share them with dream partners. Pray for clear interpretations and fitting applications—and give thanks to God!

NINE GIFTS OF THE SPIRIT

Now to each one the manifestation of the Spirit is given for the common good. To one there is given through the Spirit the message of wisdom, to another the message of knowledge by means of the same Spirit, to another faith by the same Spirit,to another gifts of healing by that one Spirit, to another miraculous powers, to another prophecy, to another distinguishing between spirits, to another speaking in different kinds of tongues, and to still another the interpretation of tongues.
- 1 Corinthians 12:7-10

We are reawakening to the fact that our God is a lavish lover with lavish gifts! These gifts build up the body and influence others for Messiah. Here is a hop, skip and jump over these gifts.

THE MESSAGE OF WISDOM

Peter had a peculiar vision of a sheet full of unclean animals, consequently he gained wisdom to join the Gentiles at Cornelius' home and see them respond to Messiah!

In a dream a former President showed me a chart displaying how one may effectively work with people by finding points of commonality among them. Subgroups may be formed by finding distinctive points of agreement. It was a gift of wisdom.

Have you been astonished by a download of solomonic wisdom? Don't claim that it comes from your own genius. May our Lord sprinkle gifts of wisdom upon you!

THE MESSAGE OF KNOWLEDGE

Jesus knew the woman at Jacob's well had five husbands and was living with a man who was not her husband. He had supernatural insight, she knew it, and responded!

I took a visiting minister to our local tavern for lunch. The waitress came by and Ron began to get words of knowledge. They came progressively. By the Spirit he saw the woman raised horses, they did barrel racing and they competed nationally. So it was! He had the woman's attention because he was listening to the Spirit.

FAITH

Everyone is given a measure of faith. God also gives special gifts of faith. Would you like some?

Paul was told by an angel that the Lord would save the lives of the people on his ship. He had faith to boldly speak to them! (Acts 27)

In July of 1987 the Lord told me, "The next miracle you see will be a resurrection from the dead." Three weeks later our daughter Theresa was abducted and drowned in a nearby irrigation ditch. When I saw her dead body faith rose up. I knew, "This is it!" You may find the story on our website at *www.landingstripenterprises.com*.

GIFTS OF HEALING

I think you ought to have a gift of healing. The world would be a happier place, and reverence Yeshua if you exercised one. Have you ever asked? Many will be relieved of vascular disease, mental illness or arthritis as you receive and act on a healing gift.

When he ascended on high, he led captives in his train and gave gifts to men.
                                        - Ephesians 4:8

After the Lord's tremendous expenditures He surely desires to see the fruit of His tribulation! We should not abort Jesus' satisfaction by failing to seek, receive and minister healing gifts.

MIRACULOUS POWERS

Multiplication of food, stilling waves and cursing fig trees - our Lord is miraculous! He intends His people to be like Him. After you have been part of miracles you can never be the same.

Paul shook off the snake into the fire. What should you shake off in Jesus' name? Sweat rags that bring healing (Acts 19:12) and praise that opens prison doors (Acts 16:25-26) are meant to inspire us to pursue miraculous gifts.

Paul said,

My message and my preaching were not with wise and persuasive words, but with a demonstration of the Spirit's power, so that your faith might not rest on men's wisdom, but on God's power.
                                        - 1 Corinthians 2:4-5

Don't wait for others. Pursue God's miraculous gifts!

PROPHECY

The woman at the conference prophesied to me that I would minister to millions primarily through the media, like radio and TV. How could an ordinary person do that? Several years later Pam and I finished an interview with a California radio station about Theresa's resurrection. I curiously asked the interviewer how many listened to their station. It was a face-slapping awakening. Millions! The prophecy was being realized!

Prophecy channels God's wisdom, courage, comfort and guidance. It opens closed doors and pulls back curtains. What an excellent tool for building up saints! Holy prophecy supercharges the Church and is a true sign for the non-believer. Seek prophetic revelation!

Follow the way of love and eagerly desire spiritual gifts, especially the gift of prophecy.
- 1 Corinthians 14:1

DISTINGUISHING BETWEEN SPIRITS

Have you ever been in a situation where you felt a sense of evil that made your skin creep or a sense of holy delight that got you jumping on your tiptoes? You were discerning. Supernatural powers of discrimination are urgently needed. Many lambs are led away by false teachings and seducing spirits because they lack it. Believers miss heaven's resources as they fail to realize an angelic presence is there to provide or guide.

I was in a library of huge books. In the dream there

were marble busts of wise and discerning people. Curiously, their noses were much larger than normal. The Lord showed me this was discernment.

You find a Tupperware dish in the back of the refrigerator. How long has it been back there? Carefully you pop the lid and give it the sniff test. Do you have a nose for discernment? Can you sense when angels or demons are about? Can you sense when things are holy or tainted? What a vital gift!

TONGUES

There was no controversy about tongues at Pentecost. There was bewilderment and amazement! I look for the day when the controversy is gone and the amazement returns. Some call speaking in tongues ecstatic utterance. On Pentecost the real biblical ecstasy was among the hearers!

> *Utterly amazed, they asked: "Are not all these men who are speaking Galileans? Then how is it that each of us hears them in his own native language?"*
> - Acts 2:7-8

The phrase "Utterly amazed" comes from existanto, the Greek related to our word ecstasy. The cosmopolitan visitors from the Mediterranean world were in "ecstasy" that these back woods, hillbilly Galileans were speaking their languages!

I love to hear of modern occurrences of saints, unacquainted with a language, who are supernaturally inspired to speak or interpret. Jesus died and rose to break the curse. One curse put on mankind, to curtail their folly, was the confusion of languages. Tongues and interpretation are gifts that undo the confusion of Babel.

There are roughly 6500 languages. The book of Revelation says the great worship service will have representatives from them all! Our gracious God dispensed tongues on Pentecost so others would learn of His Son. He still wills that those of all languages hear the message! He gives powers of communication! Let's study languages, but don't you think we should earnestly seek communication gifts which glorify God?

Many books have been written on this subject. I suggest you grab your Bible and study up.

There are inauthentic expressions of tongues. All the more reason to pursue the authentic!

I would love to set up an exercise where we get dozens of people in a line to speak in tongues and dozens of people from different language groups walking along and listening. Want to give it a try? Perhaps you should meet people, find if they are multilingual and ask if they understand your gift of tongues. I did this once under gunpoint in Turkey when our group was held up by terrorists. It's funny after the fact, but they did not understand my tongue.

Speaking in tongues is part of my personal prayer life. I would love it to be part of yours. Apparently Paul had the same attitude.

A young man came to me earnestly wanting to speak in tongues. I felt pressed for time and simply patted him on the shoulder and said, "Go home speaking in tongues!" Later he told me, as soon as he walked out the door he started speaking in tongues and did so all the way home.

If you want the gift of tongues ask your generous Father and receive it now!

INTERPRETATION OF TONGUES

...For this reason anyone who speaks in a tongue should pray that he may interpret what he says.
- 1 Corinthians 14:13

I don't know what the ratio of tongues speaker to interpreters is but I speculate it to be 200 to 1. Whatever the number, things are out of balance. The Church would be far richer if we had more interpretation gifts! Many have experienced tongues but few are prepared to interpret. We are missing inspiration we might otherwise have. What are you going to do about it?

Follow the way of love and eagerly desire spiritual gifts.
- 1 Corinthians 14:1

Addendum 3 :

"HOLY" SPIRIT

Ninety-four times in the NIV Bible the Spirit is referred to as the "Holy" Spirit. The word holy implies separate, "other" and distinct. God is not animal, mineral or vegetable. He is different. When we pray that our Father's name be regarded as holy we are asking that the astonishing, uniquely grand things about Him would stand out! This is the work of the Holy Spirit!

To be holy means to move from commonness to an exceptional place of separated distinctiveness. The Holy Spirit resting on common people makes them holy.

But you, dear friends, build yourselves up in your most holy faith and pray in the Holy Spirit.
                                                    - Jude 20

CHARACTER TRUMPS GIFTING

You may prophecy the secrets of people's hearts, but can you be trusted with a confidence? You may possess great faith, but are you arrogant? Do you use your astonishing gifts for your own advantage or to honor and build up others?

Sin will quickly compromise our ability to minister to others and hear from the Father. I would rather work with people of high character and little gifting than the other way around. Of course we pursue both! Don't minister with scummy pipes. Live a distinctive life.

Many wonder how to overcome temptation and live the victorious life. As we are filled with the Holy Spirit corrupt, carnal ways of life are stifled by a greater power! (See Galatians 5:16)

NINE FRUIT FLAVORS

But the fruit of the Spirit is love, joy, peace, patience, kindness, goodness, faithfulness, gentleness and self-control. Against such things there is no law.

- Galatians 5:22-23

There is no speed limit on joy. You won't find "No trespassing" signs for gentleness. You may be as kind or self-controlled as you wish and no one will arrest you! God the Spirit brings delicious flavors and fragrances to our communion! Some have received gifts of the Spirit but have sour dispositions. The cure is to enjoy these fruity flavors!

Addendum 4 :

IS SOMETHING MISSING?

There are at least three times in Acts where believers are missing the Holy Spirit! We should be humble enough to concede this may be our problem. Sometimes we have more form than power. There are many genuine believers who have little relationship with the Holy Spirit.

People in Samaria received the word of God through Philip but they were still missing something. Peter and John came to minister to them.

> *When they arrived, they prayed for them that they might receive the Holy Spirit, because the Holy Spirit had not yet come upon any of them; they had simply been baptized into the name of the Lord Jesus.*
>
> *- Acts 8:15-16*

Saul encountered Christ on the Damascus road. He was blinded. He believed but was not filled.

> *Then Ananias went to the house and entered it. Placing his hands on Saul, he said, "Brother Saul, the Lord Jesus, who appeared to you on the road as you were coming here has sent me so that you may see again and be filled with the Holy Spirit."*
>
> *- Acts 9:17*

Paul asked Ephesian disciples,
> *"Did you receive the Holy Spirit when you believed?*
>
> *- Acts 19:1-2*

It was not a silly question. Many believers and whole churches are dusty dry. They are waiting for a good plumber.

We owe Pentecostals and Charismatic believers a debt of gratitude. They have re-pioneered the ways of the Spirit and re-dug ancient wells. They have kept alive a passion for knowing the Spirit. While giving honor, I feel some "Spirit filled" churches are less "full" than they make themselves out to be. Sometimes I think speaking in tongues is regarded as a high-watermark which may actually limit familiarity with the Spirit. By concentrating on one beautiful manifestation of the Spirit we may miss the fact that God the Holy Spirit is immensely creative and diverse in the ways He wishes to relate to us.

On the other hand some fundamentalists, even those who call themselves "cessationists" are often more Spirit filled than they realize. They make allowances for the Holy Spirit to convict of sin and bear witness that Jesus is the only Savior. They have Spirit gumption to get out and witness. Many have faith to pray, and get answers! Those who have never seen a platypus may not believe just as those who have never seen a miracle. Many are willing to change their minds; they just are waiting for you to give them a reason.

I imagine every saint allows the Spirit to fill elements of their life but is out of touch with other areas which might be filled. We may open the door to tongues or discernment of spirits but not open the doors to visions or miracles. In addition, we may feel the power of the Spirit at 110 volts, yet never have felt 440.

We are told not to quench (1 Thessalonians 5:19) or grieve (Ephesians 4:30) the Holy Spirit but rather to stir up the gift within! (2 Timothy 1:6) We may stir a pot with a spoon or stir a fire with a stick. Wonderment will stir up worship. The fear of the Lord will stir up reverence.

Sanctified imagination stirs up vision and faith. We know some lizards grow replacement tails. Responding to a stretch of holy imagination some have believed God and seen the replacement of limbs and organs. What, after all, did our Lord Jesus mean when he said, "with God all things are possible"? (Matthew19:26) How will God be able to do more than we imagine if we fail to stir our imaginations?

THINGS WHICH FOLLOW US

If you are paddling a canoe you may turn around and see a wake is following you. Look behind a ship or even a swimmer and you will find a wake. We don't push signs and wonders, they follow us. As soon as we stop moving forward with Messiah they disappear.

Remember in the shepherd's Psalm, goodness and mercy follows us. If we are intent on following Jesus we may be confident that good things will follow. We lean forward with a view to follow Jesus, yet every so often we may take a glance in the rearview mirror, and see signs and wonders, and goodness and mercy following us!

**Follow the Lamb and He will lead you
to the Waters of Life.**

For the Lamb at the center of the throne will be their shepherd; He will lead them to springs of living water. And God will wipe away every tear from their eyes.
- Revelation 7:17

Addendum 5 :

HOSTING A RIVER SEMINAR

Host an intensive Biblically saturating
and Spiritually drenching Seminar

Experience ministry models in breakout sessions
where truth becomes experience!

DISCOVER:

- The Tangible Coming River that will spring up from the city of Jerusalem
- The Dynamic Inner River that Christ wills to flow through you
- How to Draw and Pour forth the Holy Spirit's reality as you minister to others

Host a Riverfront Property Seminar by contacting:

Steven C. Johnson
Landingstripenterprises@gmail.com

What some have said of the River Seminar:

"The conference was packed with depth and insight. Never left the edge of my seat! Let's do it again!"

- PG

"It drew people together like nothing I have experienced. Steve Johnson demonstrated the tender loving kindness of the Lord and ignited the people involved to do the same. Thank you, Holy Spirit!"

- MV

"The Riverfront Property Conference brought both empowerment and encouragement to those attending. Truly a rewarding and fulfilling experience."

- RT

"Came totally thirsty. Left totally refreshed!"

– MN

"Steve Johnson is one of the most remarkable people I have ever met. From the first time I met him I was drawn to the River of God so evident in him. I am not surprised that his book is remarkable as well. Steve writes from his own personal experience with the River Master and from the overflow of God presence flowing through him. After reading the book and experiencing the seminar I am even more hungry for the ever-increasing flow of God's presence in my life and in the city where I pastor."

Chuck Farina
Pastor of New Hope Church
Abilene, Texas

About the Author

Steve Johnson loves to go into the deep end! He aspires to stir the Church to prepare a landing strip for the Lord's return. He helps Saints discover their gifts and callings, and network in collaborative kingdom ventures. He cultivates the visions and values of His kingdom, promoting unity among believers from the micro to macro. Steve is a lover of Israel and Israel's Messiah.

He is available as an impartational guest minister and as the facilitator of Riverfront Property Seminars.

Steve is a graduate of George Fox University and Palmer Theological Seminary. He is a true pastor/teacher having served in Presbyterian, Baptist and Charismatic fellowships.

Steve and Pam Johnson live in Abilene, Texas. Steve serves on the pastoral staff at New Hope Church. They have four stellar adult children and are pleased that grandchildren are starting to show up!

Read Steven's Blog:

Landingstripenterprises.com